Tales of a Low-Rent Birder

Tales of a Low-Rent Birder

Pete Dunne

Drawings by David Sibley

Foreword by Roger Tory Peterson

Rutgers University Press / New Brunswick, New Jersey

Title page: Green-winged Teal

Copyright © 1986, by Peter Dunne

Library of Congress Cataloging-in-Publication Data

Dunne, Pete, 1951–
  Tales of a low-rent birder.

  1. Bird watching—New Jersey—Cape May. 2. Birds—
New Jersey—Cape May. I. Sibley, David. II. Title.
QL684.N5D86   1986   598'.07'23474998   85–22068
ISBN 0–8135–1139–9

Contents

Foreword
Roger Tory Peterson

Anyone who birds in New Jersey these days knows Pete Dunne, who presides over the Cape May Bird Observatory where among other duties he monitors the hawk flights.

Neither Alexander Wilson nor John James Audubon, both of whom visited and collected in southern New Jersey, knew of these flights. At Cape May, as at Hawk Mountain, the hawks were slaughtered for years before anyone became concerned. The gunner has always preceded the protectionist and the ornithologist. Fifty years ago each fall, gunners lined the concrete highway that runs from east to west just north of the resort town of Cape May Point, waiting for the hawks to come over. You could depend on the three boys who lived over the grocery store to be there, and the old Italian who ran the taxi from the railroad station, and "Pusey" who owned a boat over on the bay. Sometimes sportsmen came from as far away as Trenton and Camden.

The National Audubon Society had observers on the scene as early as 1931, and in the fall of 1935 I was sent by the Society to monitor the shooting. One morning in late September when the wind had shifted into the northwest, I watched 800 Sharp-shinned Hawks try to cross the firing line. Each time a "sharpy" sailed over the treetops it was met with a pattern of lead. Some folded up silently; others, with head wounds, flopped to the ground, chattering shrilly. By noon 254 birds lay on the pavement. That evening, in a Cape May home where I had rented a room, twenty sharp-shins were broiled like squabs for a family of six. I tasted the birds, and wondered what my friends would think if they could see me. Like a spy breaking bread with the enemy, I felt uneasy. I could not tell my hosts I disapproved, for their consciences were clear—weren't they killing the hawks as edible game and at the same time saving all the little songbirds? It would have done little good to explain predation, ecology, and the natural balance to these folk. Having lived at Cape May all their lives, they had a distorted idea of the abundance of hawks. They did not realize that a single season's sport by the Cape May gunners could drain the Sharp-shins (and other raptors) from thousands of square miles of northern woodland.

Shooting from the highways was later prohibited in New Jersey, and shooting from the wooded sandhills near Cape May Point was eliminated through the creation of the Witmer Stone Wildlife Sanctuary by the National Audubon Society. A few years later the sanctuary changed hands and was placed under the aegis of the New Jersey Audubon Society. As at Hawk Mountain, vigilance against the gunner is now a thing of the past, and education and research under the skilled guidance of Pete Dunne and his associates are today's priorities.

The observation of birds can be many things—science, an art, an esthetic experience, a game or sport, indeed anything you choose to make it. To Pete Dunne it is all of these things. He was the originator of the competitive Birdathon in the U.S.—the "World Series of Birding"—wherein several teams compete over much the same area in the state of New Jersey on the same day. To a few hardcore listers, such birding may become almost a grim do-or-die contest. Pete is not one of these. Although he can match his extremely sharp eyes and trained ears with anyone when it comes to running up a list or "getting" a rarity, he never loses his sense of fun. I know, because I accompanied Pete and his "Guerrilla Team"—Bill Boyle, Pete Bacinski, and David Sibley—on the 1984 Birdathon when we broke the New Jersey record with an all-time high of 201.

Not everyone is turned on by birding, but hundreds of thousands are; it is one of the fastest growing recreations or sports in our country. To me it has become an obsession from which I have never freed myself. Therefore I thoroughly understand

Pete Dunne; he finds joy in every moment he is able to spend watching birds.

With a background in political science and a flair for PR, Pete Dunne is very articulate, able to write about his adventures in a highly entertaining way. Days afield, whether at Cape May or elsewhere, are never run-of-the-mill. To him there is no such thing as a "ho-hum" bird; even a robin or a jay may be the focus of a hilarious or mind-boggling experience. Read what he has to say about birds and the birders who pursue them with such a passion.

Preface

The stories in this book were written between 1977 and 1985. They appeared in the *Peregrine Observer* newsletter—with little thought about how they might (or might not) fit together between hard covers. A fair number resurfaced in places like *Bird Watcher's Digest* and *New Jersey Audubon*. A few nagging scraps of memory suggest that there may have been one or two spot appearances in several other journals or newsletters.

Even though each story deals with a separate theme or event, they have at least two things in common. They all deal at least peripherally with Cape May, New Jersey (which is such a marvelous place that you wonder why it isn't somewhere else) and they center around some facet of birds or birding. Do you have to be a birdwatcher in order to enjoy them? I don't think so—but I'm hardly in a position to judge. Assessing the merits of stories is the reader's right and privilege. I wouldn't presume to interfere.

And, I won't.

Some of the people mentioned in these pages are as real as you and I, friends and acquaintances; people that it has been my fortune to know. Others are conjured from half-truths or fancy—but I wouldn't be quick to categorize them if I were you. The birding community is populated by an improbable host of characters. Some of them (God knows) don't have far to go to transcend the bounds of credibility.

There are a few people who aren't mentioned in these pages and to rob them of recognition would be an indiscretion beyond all bearing. People like—Earl Marlatt, Floyd Wolfarth,

Donna McDowell, Clay Sutton, Susan Taylor, Karen Nolan, Michael Heller, Pete Olshefski, Cynthia Slack, Jane Tanaskovic, Bill and Elsa Thompson, Mary Bowers, and my parents, who had a hand in the preparation of these stories and whose influence, somewhere down the line, guided the hand of the writer.

And there are two other people that I'd like to cut from the pack. One is Linda Mills, who will worry a manuscript to death—until the last dangling modifier is ferreted out.

The other is Robert Burke.

Cape May Point, NJ
15 April 1985

This book is dedicated to Robert Burke
(because it will shock hell out of him)

Tales of a Low-Rent Birder

Billy Leeds and the Eagle

The sound of an approaching car stopped me mid-scan—and small wonder! Old salt hay roads on open marsh aren't heavily trafficked as a rule. In fact, with the exception of crabbers, gunners in season, and an occasional researcher, they aren't much used at all. Except, of course, in August, at harvest, when the lush salt hay is cut and baled; a ritual whose essential elements have not changed since Blackbeard sailed the waters of Delaware Bay.

Resisting the impulse to look up, I let my ears feel the situation out. No sense in looking suspicious. The engine chugged heavily but it lacked the throaty heft of a pickup. I figured it for a sedan or wagon, certainly domestic, undeniably vintage, eight cylinders (missing on one, maybe two). It sounded like the kind of lovable old wreck that has had everything replaced at least once and, having accepted the futility of further resistance, just runs on now if only because it would take too much energy to do otherwise.

I guessed it was a Chevy on the basis of abundance and range.

A distant Turkey Vulture gave me an object on which to feign studied interest. I stepped just a little farther off the elevated roadbed as the approach drew near.

A grinding rumble heralded, simultaneously, touchdown and severely worn brakes. A loud screech of metal on metal followed by a sharp bang told me a door had opened, only one door. It was time to turn around.

My audio analysis was pretty much on the money. The car *was* vintage, one of those high-finned atrocities that went out

with the Eisenhower administration; but Buick, not Chevy
(same genus, different species). The color, at some point, might
have been blue. Now it was two-toned, rust and gray. There
was little time for study. What emerged from the dispirited old
wreck was just as curious.

Using every advantage afforded by leverage, gravity, and mo-
mentum, and amid a flurry of cuss words whose color and ca-
dence spoke of many years of practice, the driver worked himself out of the car. With the startling speed of a fiddler crab he

Soaring harriers

sidled to within three feet of me, cocked his head slightly, and regarded me hostilely.

He was not tall, though he might have been, once; he was lean and toothless. The kind of person you'd call a character. I have no memory of his clothes. They suited him, whatever they were, and this means that they must have been the standard bayshore issue: slacks and short-sleeved shirt, threadbare and sunbleached. His arms, thin and heavily veined, hung motionless from shoulders that held a permanent droop. His face was long and thin, pixie-like, tanned in blotches. Oddly, it was free of wrinkles, except around the eyes. The eyes were crinkled nicely, no doubt from many years spent looking into the sun. They gave him the suggestion of a squint.

But the eyes themselves were blue, like an August afternoon sky when the sun has burned the color out of it. They sparkled like broken glass and there was more than a touch of madness in them.

He was an old, old man.

But he got right to the point.

"Wha' ya doin' heah?"

I knew he wasn't the landowner. I'd already spoken with him. But under the circumstances it really didn't matter. He was quite obviously a local, and on the Cumberland bayshore this means to have roots that go back very far. He could probably trace his genealogy back through eight generations encompassing gentry and market gunners, dirt farmers and oystermen, ministers and smugglers, sea captains and shingle miners. No doubt his ancestors had lived on the bayshore back when beating authority meant dodging the King's dragoons. And, of course, that gave him standing to confront me on the open marsh. I was an outsider, born elsewhere and beyond redemption. But I had learned a thing or two in my trips to the bayshore, about the people and how to get along with them.

"Lookin' fer chicken hawks," I replied, falling into his speech pattern.

"Chicken hawks!?" he said. It was both a question and statement. "YeeeEh," he continued, "chicken hawks! Shoot 'em every chance I git!"

3

He tipped his head a little more to the side and regarded me slyly, testing me.

Yes, I'd learned a thing or two. "Yeah," I agreed, "they're mean all right. Kill a lot of game, do they?"

"Do they?" he exclaimed. "Why, I seen 'em kill whole families of ducks, bigguns and littleuns, one right after 'nuther. An' rabbits! Kill so many rabbits ain't hardly worth gunnin' 'em any more." He paused, thinking back. "I saw one kill a goose, once," he added, and then stopped, glaring at me, daring me to question it.

I didn't.

Now, in case this discussion of predator-prey relationships leaves you guessing as to the identity of the raptor in question, the bird is the Northern Harrier—the Marsh Hawk, *Circus cyaneus.* Along the bayshore, this is the *chicken hawk,* though some insist that the term can be appropriately applied to all raptors. Lumpers are not a new phenomenon.

The observations of my friend notwithstanding, there have been an awful lot of studies done on the prey items of harriers, and although availability has a great deal to do with what is taken, most experts agree that small mammals are the mainstay in the bird's diet; songbirds assume secondary preference. I know of accounts in which harriers have taken rabbits and attacked waterfowl up to the size of hen Canvasback (without success) but I have never seen a harrier grab anything larger than a Clapper Rail. All this, of course, is not to say that my aquaintance did not see a harrier kill a goose. Certainly not! Under the circumstances, I gave it the lowest possible form of acceptance, subject to later evaluation and dismissal.

"My name's Billy Leeds," he said, suddenly. "Lived here all my life." He looked away, quickly, seeing things that can only be seen through the filter of a man's mind, and then just as quickly looked back.

"How old d'ya think I am?" he asked.

I undershot. "Seventy-five?"

"Ha!" he laughed (delighted by the figure). "Ha! I'm ninety-two. Yessir, ninety-two last winter, an' I live here all my life."

He looked away again, and then quickly back.

"Di'ja git any?"

"Excuse me?" I said—and kicked myself. "*What?*" would have been the proper reply.

He ignored the indiscretion. "Di'ja git any chicken hawks?"

"Oh, chicken hawks," I repeated, stupidly, "no, not a one."

This seemed to touch a responsive chord in Billy's mind. He reached for the memory.

"Last winter," he began, "I seen a big black chicken hawk. Beeeg sucker! Beeeg sucker! Biggest, blackest chicken hawk you ever seen. Ain't many around as used to be."

Maybe he saw me stiffen, but I think not. Billy was lost in the memory of it, looking off across the marsh and seeing it again. From what Billy had said, the bird could only have been an eagle and the odds say an immature Bald Eagle. Immature birds lack the white heads and tails of adults. The marshes of Delaware Bay have a small wintering population, a pitiful remnant of what there used to be, just as Billy said.

"He was right over there," Billy continued, moving one of his arms vaguely to the east, "sitting right down on the marsh. I reach fer my gun," he said, his voice taut with the excitement and the memory.

And I saw it happen, too; the young bird, inexperienced, knowing nothing of men, their motives, and the long reach of their judgment; and Billy, motivated by an assurance beyond question that the hawk was bad and killing it was good. A belief inherited as a birthright, now reinforced by ninety-two years. It might not have been true—it *isn't* true—but to Billy it was right.

There have been many instances in this age of man when fact has gone head to head with belief. Sometimes it loses.

"I reach fer my gun," Billy said, but then he paused and seemed, somehow, to diminish before my eyes like a banner when the wind fails. "But I was too slow," he said, finally, softly, and then he looked back over the marsh again as he seemed to ponder the meaning of this.

Just as Billy is a product of his time, I am a product of mine. A naturalist, researcher, and Audubon Society Naturalist Director. I have known the friendship of Maurice Broun, perhaps the greatest raptor protector that the world has ever seen. I know much about predators and their role, and I believe that it is wrong, aside from being illegal, to kill hawks and owls, and my belief is founded in fact. I am twenty-nine.

And then there is Billy Leeds, ninety-two, who has seen many chicken hawks and "shoots 'em every chance he gits." And I weighed my knowledge against Billy's ninety-two years. What should I say?

Billy was looking out over the marshes, arms at his sides, head cocked at that funny angle. And I looked at the long, full-veined limbs, the eyes that sparkled but had lost their youth, and recalled the voice firm with conviction.

And I said, "That's too bad, Mr. Leeds. Maybe you'll get another chance."

Overflight

"Everybody have their seat belt fastened?"

We did. After three weeks, we knew the routine.

Our pilot fiddled convincingly with several rows of important looking switches and dials, rapped soundly on one that was not to his liking—and then ignored the whole bright array. Say what you will about Hank, he was no slave to gadgetry.

Wade, our project leader, sat in the copilot's seat. Teddy and I sat in the back. We were conducting weekly surveys along the New Jersey side of Delaware Bay. Our target was migratory shorebirds, the tens upon tens of thousands of shorebirds that use Delaware Bay each spring as the jump-off point for the last leg of their journey to tundra breeding grounds. How many shorebirds? Nobody really knew. And nobody really knew exactly how to go about finding out, either. Enter Cape May Bird Observatory. Enter . . .

Hank swung the single-engine Piper Warrior about, requesting takeoff instructions. What came back sounded like a Munchkin with a mouth full of mothballs speaking some arcane Xhosa dialect inside a wind tunnel.

Maybe Hank actually understood what was being said (or at least enough to get by). More likely, he gave about as much importance to verbal instructions as he did to instrument panels. After all, there wasn't anybody in our way and the engine *was* running.

We taxied to the end of the runway and swung around to face the long strip of macadam that would be our mainline to

Shorebirds dancing and weaving to confound the steel falcon

heaven (figuratively speaking). Everything seemed up to specs: my binoculars, Wade's pencil, Hank's airplane.

"Piper Warrior two-five-zero requesting permission to take off."

"Ahhhhrrrr-Raaahgaaahh . . . Ahh thare-uh Tooh-Fy-Ow. Yuaave-Kleeah . . . (snap)."

"Roger."

" —act . . . (snap)."

This seemed to satisfy Hank. At least, he started down the runway. And with an enthusiasm that belied his many hours flight time and several consecutive nights in Wildwood's bars, Hank got the plane airborne.

As the earth fell away from us, the peninsula took form. The lighthouse gleamed brightly a scant four miles south. To the north, the bayshore stretched like a ribbon of green peace, and below, the Villas sprawled in structured, suburban order. Beyond was the Bay.

It was two hours to low on a falling tide. The wide flats off the beach were a braided series of channels and sand bars. As we cleared the town, Hank throttled down and made a wide, arching swing that brought us down to one hundred feet over the water and two hundred yards offshore heading north. The stall speed indicator buzzed angrily. Hank throttled up a hair and the buzzing became intermittent. We were into birds almost immediately.

"Small flock on the bar there, Wade," I piped in my best researcher voice. "Got 'em?"

"Doing a running count," he said in tones that suggested that there could be no other answer. "Peep . . . sanderling mostly."

I ran my binoculars along the shoreline, picking up birds as I went.

"Got Sanderling on the beach. I'll give you a count."

"400 . . . 425 . . . . Right," Wade snapped. "Big flock getting up under us."

I looked in time to see a sandbar sprout wings and rise into motion beneath and then behind us. The birds settled almost immediately.

9

"Get 'em?" asked Wade.

"Missed 'em," I replied. "Back one time, Hank?"

The throttle opened up and an invisible hand pushed us back into our seats. The horizon cut the windshield at an uncomfortable sixty degree angle.

We did better this time. Wade went for a total, counting in lots of one hundred. For larger groups, he counted in lots of one thousand. My job was to study the species composition of each flock and break it down into percentages. Both tasks take intense concentration, a little discipline, and some on-the-job training.

This flock was fairly uniform. The bulk of the birds were small (peep). Here and there you could pick out a broad wing stripe in the melee (Sanderling), but most of the wings at forty yards and seventy miles per hour looked pretty solid (Semipalmated Sandpipers). Mixed in with the peep was a larger species of shorebird. Their gleaming white underparts identified them as Ruddy Turnstones. This is gestalt birding honed to laser perfection.

"About 2,300 birds," Wade pronounced.

"Give it 75% Semis, 10 Sand and 15 RUTU," I added.

Wade nodded, writing as I spoke.

We approached Dias Creek, the site of our first major concentration. The sand below the high-tide line erupted in a low, flowing wave of cinnamon and silver: Knot! The birds curled seaward, instinctively seeking the safety of open space. They passed beneath the plane, banked softly, and alighted on the beach. Feeding commenced immediately. Even from one hundred feet, we could see the lines of deposited horseshoe crab eggs set like mineral veins in smooth white marble, virtually an unlimited food supply. The tiny loaves that feed the multitudes.

Wade counted silently, his attention focused upon cutting the rising ribbon into 1,000-bird lengths. My part was easy, this time. The analysis came up nearly pure Red Knot.

Wade wrote 8,000 on the pad.

Birds came faster now. Isolated groups lost their sovereignty to a running count.

At Reed's Beach tight groups of turnstones exploded into flight like firecrackers on a string. At the mouth of Goshen Creek, another traditional hotspot, three large groups of turnstones and knots rose simultaneously, giving form to the wind. They merged, turned, and separated—dancing and weaving a pattern contrived to confound the steel falcon screaming down on them from out of the sun. It was awesome and confusing and it undermined concentration. Putting a number to the whole was as difficult as cutting a single out of the flock. The temptation was strong to simply pick a number out of the air and put it down. To try to capture the wind by putting numbers to it seemed superficial and irrelevant.

But we tried, anyway, because we were trained to, because it was important that we do so, and because some day this information might be used to save the lives of the birds that give form to the wind. If a number cannot convey the wonder of it, at least it cannot diminish it.

So we counted.

"A 40/40 split on turnstone and knot," I announced. "Balance: peep."

"Yeeeup," piped Wade. "Twenty-five thousand birds on that stretch of beach. Twenty-five."

We ran along empty bayshore for a time. The waves licked at the dark sod bank that dropped sharply into the peat-stained water. There were no beaches here, no place for crabs to deposit their tribute of eggs—and no birds. There were only gulls and, running out from the waves, the timeless marshes of Delaware Bay.

We were coming up on Moore's Beach now, a two-mile strip of sand and a cluster of stick-borne houses that are the hallmark of bayshore communities and of people who have learned to live with the tide so that it governs the rhythm of their own lives. I could feel the tension rising in Wade. Moore's Beach was a hotspot.

From a distance, there was nothing to see, no telltale shading of light and dark areas that would have heralded clusters of birds. There was just unbroken uniformity, and common sense told us that the beaches were empty. My mind repeated the thought to gain assurance: *"The beach is empty."* We leaned forward anyway, because the beach *couldn't* be empty. Last week there had been 20,000 birds here. And this was the peak of the migration. It couldn't be empty. But the alternative would be . . . that is, the beach would have to be . . . but *that* would be impossible!

And as the distance fell away below us, there was nothing left but to accept, somehow, a reality that stood beyond and apart from any in our experience.

"THERE IS NO BEACH. THERE ARE ONLY BIRDS HERE."

Nothing had prepared us for *this*. No discipline of mind, no perfection of method, and certainly no resource of experience.

I am no stranger to numbers of birds. I have seen swallows at Cape May Point in numbers that reduced the amount of sunlight reaching the earth. I have seen Sharp-shinned Hawks riding the dunes at Higbee Beach at the rate of one every second and I have seen Snow Geese at Heislerville that rose like storm clouds on a Dakota sky. But I had never seen anything like this.

We tried to count them, and our resolve passed through them like bullets through smoke. The ocean of birds rose and fanned out in waves that swept around us. In seconds, the plain, simple weight of numbers humbled us into the role of spectators.

"I guess we'd better go around again" was all Wade could say.

We did better this time, knowing what we were up against (and staying a little farther offshore), cutting the mass mentally into manageable blocks and percentages. And then we did it one more time, just to make certain.

Seventy thousand birds: forty thousand Sanderling, thirty thousand turnstone. We swung offshore for a breather—to collect our thoughts, get our figures straight, and shake our heads in disbelief.

The Heislerville mud flats vibrated as with Brownian motion, teeming with feeding Semipalmated Sandpipers. As we turned for a second run over Basket Flat, Teddy brought his glasses up casually, studied a large salt marsh pond for a pensive few seconds and announced, "Black-necked Stilt."

"What?!"

Hank banked hard to the tune of a deranged stall speed indicator, and while he struggled to keep his plane up, we fought desperately to keep our lunches down. And, sure enough, there, calmly picking its way along the shallows, was one of New Jersey's most uncommon shorebirds.

We cleared Ben Davis Point, turning northwest. A massive gyrating free-for-all of shorebirds flushed wildly ahead of the plane; knot, turnstone, and peep. Some headed back down along the course we'd already come and if they'd gotten away, we'd lose them in birds already censused. Hank banked hard to keep the escaping flocks in sight, losing altitude steadily. The stall speed indicator screeched defiantly. But we got 'em, all of them, and as we looked up, relief evident on all of our faces, we noticed that there was something in our way.

It was the town of Fortescue.

Miracles still happen on this earth. They are not as common, as a rule, as they used to be, but they still happen now and again. Hank brought the plane's nose up *fast*, but bringing the nose up and making the rest of an airplane follow suit is not axiomatic—not at stall speed, anyway. No, I think we got some lift from an outside source on this one. And somewhere on the outskirts of Fortescue, there is still a resident puzzling over the set of wheel marks rising vertically on a clean white sheet.

Several people have asked me whether I was ever, well, *anxious* while flying the surveys. In truth, I wasn't. I mean, I was watching and Hank was flying. I figured if we ever crashed, I wasn't responsible.

Fortescue was the last of the major concentration points. Oh, we ran into other birds as we continued up the bay, but none to compare to the numbers lying south and east of Fortescue. There were 318,000 shorebirds on the bayshore on May 27, 1981—almost a third of a million. If as many birds were to be found on the vast mud flats on the Delaware side of the bay, that would make more than 600,000 birds. Included in our day's tally were 62,000 Red Knot, 96,000 Ruddy Turnstone, and 162,000 peep.

Numbers. Just abstractions without substance, like the wind without birds.

A Tale of Two Hawkwatchers

1931

Eric woke to the sound of his mother shaking ashes from the stove, just as he had the morning before, and the morning before that, and every morning that he could remember in his sixteen years. He dressed hurriedly in the dark, partly because of the cold, partly because of the excitement. There would be a flight at Cape May Point, today. Hawks would be skimming the treetops: hundreds of them, maybe thousands. Normally he worked Saturdays but he had asked for and been given the day off.

It had surprised him a little that he had gotten off so easily. The foreman at the fish docks had cussed some and gone on for a time about how much tougher life was when *he* was a boy. But he relented anyway, and sooner than usual. It was a thing Eric had noticed. People seemed to go a little out of the way for him since the *Laura B.* went down.

Hugging the wall and avoiding the boards that creaked so as not to wake his brothers, Eric negotiated the stairs with practiced steps. A large plate of hotcakes awaited him in the kitchen. He attacked it singlemindedly and downed scalding coffee as fast as the limits of pain would allow.

His mother watched him over her own cup with soft gray eyes that never betrayed anger or kindness. He'd inherited those eyes—but the unkempt mane of red hair and the freckles that overran both cheeks and formed a bridge over his nose had been a gift from his father.

"Dress warm," she said. "The wind'll drive the cold into you."

Eric nodded in affirmation, mouth full of coffee.

"I packed a sandwich. It's near yer boots."

Eric's mumbled thanks echoed hollow in the mug.

The silver bell on the gun rack door rang sharp and cold in the dark despite his cautious effort. His father had put it there when Eric was a toddler—a precaution against the curious hands of children. Eric reached reflexively for his gun but hesitated as his fingers touched the stock.

It was a fine old gun, a Parker double. The bluing on the barrel had long since given way to rust. The stock was cracked near the grip from some forgotten mishap. An earlier owner had wound brass wire around it for support. Eric had bought this gun with his first earnings at Snow's fish dock and he had carried it for three seasons. But now his hand strayed down the line of metal and wood that glowed softly in the half-light cast by the kitchen door, past the carbine his grandfather had carried through the "war of rebellion," past the Springfield his father had carried through France, past other guns of lesser lineage. It came to rest upon the twelve-gauge.

It was a beautiful gun, his father's prize. Five shots, fast as a man could squeeze the trigger, chambered for standard loads or

Handcounter and shotgun shells

three-inch magnums, a lasting tribute to the genius of its inventor, John M. Browning.

He had fired it once before, and poorly. The stock was too long, cut to a bigger man's frame. But that was two years ago. He had the frame, now—though the man that was to fill it was still several years away.

Eric lifted the gun free, felt the supreme lightness, caught the sweet smell of solvent that still clung to the barrel a year after it had last been cleaned. His mother watched from the kitchen door. Her eyes betrayed nothing.

The stars glittered like shards of ice as Eric turned down Washington Street onto Sunset Boulevard. The wind tore the frosted breath from his lips. It was a three-mile walk to the end of Sunset where the line of gunners would be waiting. The hawks would begin to fly at first light and would move south along the length of the peninsula. They would turn west when confronted by the open bay and then, like baitfish in a wier, curl north along the shore, following the contours of the bay. The birds would be low now, and hugging the treetops, their progress slowed by gusty headwinds. And they wouldn't be able to see the line of gunners waiting for them on the concrete road that cut across their path until they broke into the open—until it was too late.

The guns would roar, shots coming so fast that it sounded like one long, endless roll of thunder. His grandfather used to liken it to the Union artillery at Vicksburg. And the hawks would fall to the roadway. Some would tumble like a football, end over end. Some would arch like a catcher's throw to second. A lot of birds that weren't hit clean would fly weakly into the trees on the gunners' side of the road. They would starve eventually, or the foxes would get them.

By afternoon on a good day, there would be a large pile of hawks at the end of Sunset Boulevard. The local papers would take pictures. The gunners would stand behind mounds of fresh-shot birds and smile for the camera. Cars driving down the road had to shift to low gears to keep from skidding on the spent shells scattered on the roadbed. It was really something.

There were some gunners who said that *all* hawks were bad

and should be shot. But Eric knew better. He liked birds, studied them whenever he could, and read about them in books from his grandfather's library. He particularly liked the yellow-eyed fish hawk that nested so commonly on the Cape. He loved to watch the adults and newly fledged young mounting higher and higher over summer marshes, and he loved to watch them plunge into the bay for weakfish (even though it made the commercial fishermen mad).

But the blue darter was a bad hawk. There was no denying that. They killed songbirds. They were so quick that the little birds didn't have a chance. He had learned from the big, two-volume book about New York birds that the scientific name *Accipiter velox* meant "swift hawk," and that when a Sharp-shinned caught a bird it would take it to a butchering block. He remembered that Eaton, the *orthinologist*, said that you could always tell a butcher block when you found one because of all the feathers around it. He had never seen a butcher block but he had often seen rings of feathers scattered in the woods of Cape May where Sharp-shinneds had eaten a kill. Yes, they were "bloodthirsty little pirates," just like Eaton and the other orthinologists said—and "should be destroyed" (Eaton said that, too).

But that didn't go for all hawks. Only Sharp-shinneds and Cooper's and Goshawks and Duck Hawks were destructive and not protected now. Killing Sharp-shinneds saved lots of songbirds, but there was another good reason to shoot them. Eric could get a nickel apiece for birds that weren't shot up too bad. Sharp-shinneds made pretty good eating. They tasted like chicken. Shells cost two for a nickel, so if he was shooting good, he could make over two cents for each bird he killed.

Of course, misses cut into the profit margin.

The street began to dance in the headlights thrown from a car coming up from behind. The car slowed as it drew abreast and a man's voice inquired: "Going to the shoot, son?"

"Yes, sir," Eric replied, recognizing the voice as belonging to the editor of a local paper.

"Well, hop in then. Hand your gun to Phil there in the back."

Eric complied and noted with equal measures of pride and

embarrassment Phil's admiring appraisal of his gun and the care with which he set it next to the other guns propped in the back seat.

"Nice looking shotgun you have there," he said, addressing Eric. "Any chicken hawk with a sense of honor should take one look at it and just surrender to you."

"Well, I guess you better go and get one for yourself, then, Phil," chided the driver. "'way you shoot, the only way you're going to put a bird in your game bag is if he flies in there himself."

"Ha, ha, ha. Ha, ha, ha."

"Why Frank, I thought that's why you brought me along. You were goin' to drive and I was goin' to shoot 'cause you drive a darn sight better than you shoot and you can't drive worth a damn."

"Ha, ha, ha. Ha, ha, ha."

Gun talk. Men talk. It was a thing that Eric had grown up with. It was all part of fall at Cape May.

The headlights showed other cars and twenty or so men and boys at the end of Sunset, jacketed figures cloaked in anonymity by distance and darkness that fell away as the car drew near. Most were local people Eric knew or recognized. Here and there red plaid jackets marked the "sports" down from Philadelphia. The shoots were getting popular with the sporting crowd.

Light was beginning to gather the sky over the lighthouse. The stars had lost their sparkle. The clump of men drew gradually into a line flanking the road. Eric took a place at one end. He reached into his pocket, removed a shell, and pushed it through the floor plate of the Magnum 5. The mechanism snatched it impatiently from his fingers and guided it smoothly into the chamber, ready to fire. The gliding sound of metal on metal rang softly in the air. Four more shells followed the first.

Along the line, men moved their feet restlessly, but whether from nervousness or cold it was hard to say. Their eyes were turned toward the trees flanking the far side of the road, their faces drained of life by the gray light of morning.

For the first time since his arrival, Eric noticed the figure standing off to one side. He didn't have a gun, just binoculars, but he was watching the tree line just as intently as the line of gunners. Phil noticed Eric's interest and hastened over to explain.

"He's a warden hired by the *Aw-doo-bon* Society—name of Saunders. He's makin' sure nobody guns any *ill-legal* hawks. He's even trying to count all the hawks that go by. Can you imagine anyone tryin' to count all these hawks?"

Eric studied the man with heightened interest. He'd never met anyone from the Audubon Society before. The man, Saunders, turned to regard the line of gunners, noticed Eric's gaze, and nodded in a friendly fashion. Eric returned the nod and considered going over to say hello.

A shot rang down the line followed by two more in quick succession. A Sharp-shinned Hawk, naked against the morning sky, crumbled and was swallowed by the dark backdrop of trees. Scattered cheers broke out.

Eric fixed his attention on the treetops, finger on the safety, gun held at ready. He flicked a quick glance at the Audubon warden and saw him write something on a pad. Then his eye caught movement out ahead of him.

The gun came up quick and smooth. Cheek pressed firmly on the stock, Eric swung the barrel—turning from the waist, moving the muzzle along the path of the bird. The Sharp-shinned folded its wings and began to quarter to the right in a shallow dive. Eric followed, and as the muzzle moved ahead of the bird, he pulled the trigger . . .

1981

. . . "I'll break their heads!" Carol muttered softly in the slow, even monotones that denote real anger in a person. Two more shots followed the first. Pellets, their energy spent, pattered harmlessly on and around the roof of the Higbee Beach Field Station. Carol opened her eyes with an effort, glowered at the roof—at nothing in particular—and repeated murderously,

"I'll break their heads. So help me, if those guys are shooting woodcock in the no-fire zone again, I'll feed them to vultures."

Wisely, the gunners held their fire.

Carol drew herself deeper into her polarguard bag and luxuriated in the warmth, reluctant to leave it. For almost two months now she had risen before dawn, walked the short distance to the hawk watch tower at Higbee Beach Wildlife Management Area, and recorded the numbers of migratory raptors passing through. It was part of a project to understand the raptor use of the Higbee tract. For two months, she had been at her post for ten hours a day, seven days a week, identifying and recording the sixteen species of raptors that make up the Cape May flights; noting, hourly, all pertinent weather and flight-related variables; answering the queries of passing birders and hunters; and, each evening, transcribing field notes onto the impersonal and inflexible likes of computer-ready data forms.

And for the past several weeks, she had been moonlighting at the owl nets by helping to run checks and process captures. And now she was very, very tired. More tired than she had ever been in her twenty-three years.

The light seeping into the room served notice that it was past time to go to work. Carol eased one foot experimentally from the seductive confines of the sleeping bag and, like the good field researcher she was, tested to see whether the world was where she had left it several hours before. She didn't want to leap to any indefensible conclusions.

Her foot intersected a hard, flat plane, which she tentatively identified as the floor. Carol sighed. The world was still there, all right. She didn't press her luck with further experimentation. One of the first things you learn as a biologist is *never* to repeat an experiment successfully concluded. You might not be able to duplicate the results.

Carol dressed hurriedly, partly because of the cold and partly because she was late. She stumbled noisily out to the kitchen, clear across the trailer, and proceeded to smear with a soup spoon large globs of one hundred percent natural peanut butter onto whole wheat bread.

All the knives were in the sink.

As she munched, hurriedly, on what passes for breakfast on a hawkwatcher's salary, she leafed through several day's accumulation of mail. There was a letter from a popular bimonthly magazine telling her that she may already have won twenty-five thousand dollars, a letter from the finance company advising her that another college loan payment was due, a catalogue from one of those Colorado-based manufacturers of hyper-quality backpacking gear filled with equipment bearing price tags that anybody who actually uses the stuff cannot possibly afford, and, finally, a letter from New Jersey Civil Service advising her of the hiring freeze for nongame biologists.

The usual fare.

At the trailer door, she reached fondly for her trusty old binoculars and ran a finger lightly along their length. It was a fine old pair of binos, a Bushnell Insta-focus. The enamel on both barrels had long since given way to bare metal. The focus lever had cracked near the base in some best-forgotten misadventure. A little Super glue, judiciously applied, had given it several more years of life. Carol had bought this pair with her first earnings as an assistant manager at Arthur Treacher's Fish and Chips during her freshman year. She had carried them for eight semesters and one season at Cape May.

But now her hand strayed over to the soft leather case that glowed amber in the half-light of morning. The metal clasp snapped sharp and cold; the case disclosed a beautiful pair of Nikon binoculars, her prize possession—eight power with a field of 325 feet at one thousand yards, boasting a light gathering index of fifteen, a lasting tribute to the manufacturing and marketing genius of Japanese optics.

Carol lifted the binoculars free from the case and felt their supreme lightness (and caught the sweet smell of honey that still clung to the barrels after last evening's mishap at dinner).

Treacherous stuff, honey.

The clouds, rushing low overhead, were washed in lavender and salmon as Carol moved down New England Road toward the hawk watch tower. Hawks were already beginning to pass overhead, their progress slowed to a crawl by strong headwinds. Her hands moved reflexively for the counters nestled deep in the pockets of her parka. The soft gliding sound of metal on metal sounded hollow in the three-inch loft of goose down. Each muffled "click" marked the passage of another bird: Sharp-shinned Hawks in the right hand, kestrels in the left, the birds that account for sixty-six percent of the Higbee Beach flight.

Carol climbed the tower with the easy grace of a born athlete, something that even several layers of winter clothing couldn't disguise. She had been All-State in three sports in high school but had elected to pursue a career in environmental studies instead of Phys. Ed. Raptors had become her obsession during her undergraduate days at East Stroudsburg State—four years spent in the shadow of the Kittatinny Ridge, the most famous raptor corridor in North America.

She had learned all the tenets of contemporary ornithological thought postulated by Ian Newton, Leslie Brown, the Craighead brothers, and others. She had learned much about predators and the role of predation in the maintenance of a balanced environment. She knew that raptor populations were contingent upon many things, including the abundance of prey—that no species of raptor can increase beyond the carrying capacity of its prey base. She had learned that birds of prey may be used as an environmental litmus paper to test the health and stability of the whole natural structure. And she knew that birds of prey, like all creatures, have needs that must be met. Unless man is mindful of these needs, his actions may undermine them. Carol's project at Higbee Beach was part of an effort to understand the needs of the thousands of hawks that migrate through Cape May, New Jersey.

There was another thing about the way Carol moved that went beyond simple coordination and conditioned reflexes. There was an air of satisfaction about her, the kind that comes of believing that what you are doing has purpose. Carol is a professional hawkwatcher, a rare breed among mankind. Nobody watches hawks for the money. There isn't any. People become hawkwatchers because they love it. At the end of the season she will find a job inside or outside her field to tide her over. During that time, she will wait impatiently for spring—and the Sandy Hook Hawk Watch that begins in March.

Someday, there might be grad school, or a desk job, or a family, or any one of the many trappings of life. But for now, for Carol, there was only the flight—and being part of autumn at Cape May.

From her platform thirty-five feet over Higbee, she could see most of the area south of the Cape May canal. The birds moved through in pulses like blood from the heart. Several birders were searching the sorghum for sparrows; two groups of hunters were running their dogs in the woods for woodcock.

A small figure wearing a faded plaid jacket and carrying a shotgun that looked to be about two sizes too big for him worked his way up the hedge, toward the tower. Carol noted appreciatively that he carried the gun with the muzzle facing away from the tower. It looked like a gun that had seen a lot of seasons.

A new wave of birds began moving through well left of the tower. Carol brought her binoculars up quick and smooth; the Sharp-shinned counter cradled in her right hand pressed firmly against her cheek. She moved the glasses along the path of birds and clicked off Sharpies as fast as they passed through her field. A voice hailed her from below.

"Hey, what'cha doin'?"

Carol looked down into a pair of inquisitive gray eyes set against an unkempt mane of red hair and freckles that overran both cheeks to form a bridge over the fellow's nose.

"Countin' hawks," she replied, looking quickly back to the flight to pick up a few stragglers.

"Good Sharp-shinned flight today, isn't it?" the young fella invited.

Carol looked back down at him with heightened interest.

"You like watching hawks?" she inquired.

"Yeah," he replied, "I like all birds, especially Fish Hawks—I mean Osprey. I saw one about five minutes ago up the road a ways. Did you get it?"

Carol stiffened defensively, her professional pride injured.

The young hunter noticed this. "It might have been just a gull," he offered. "It was a long way off. They look an awful lot alike."

"Yeah, they sure do," Carol agreed.

"Well, I gotta get going. Good luck."

"Yeah, you too," Carol said.

She turned her eyes back to the main flight path and picked up a harrier moving low near the wood's edge, several more distant Sharpies, and a bird at the limit of conjecture that took on more and more of the characteristics of a Cooper's Hawk the closer it got, confirming her suspicions. The Cooper's Hawk made her feel good. It was a call that most people wouldn't be able to make.

She looked after the retreating figure and on impulse hailed his back.

"Hey, what's your name?"

The young hunter turned and smiled. "Eric," he said.

Pulling Strings

I make one survey of the South Cape May Meadows every day. There is a Least Tern colony that needs checking and Curlew Sandpipers that need discovering. Life needs purpose.

Anyway, that is what I was doing when I found the string. Great stuff, string. You can do so much with it: follow it, roll it into a ball, hoard it, tie it around fingers, old newpapers, boxes filled with baked goods. Over time, these many specialized functions have given rise to strings specialized to cater to these special uses.

It was my practiced opinion that what I had discovered was string of a sort one normally associates with kites. It was in the proper habitat. One end led over the dunes to the beach— prime kite habitat. The other end trailed out into the open meadow. My experience has led me to understand that attached to one end of a kite string (normally the distal end) is a kite. Though none could be seen, I was confident that a kite was somewhere in the vicinity. I decided to test my assumption and to prove the existence of a kite.

Two courses of action seemed plausible. The first was to follow the string. The second was to give it a tug. I opted for the second on the grounds that (a) it was easier (b) I could tug both ends at once by lifting vertically, whereas if I opted for the first course of action, I would still have to decide which end to follow.

That's the problem with finding the middle of a piece of string.

If I followed the end that led out into the marsh, I stood a very good chance of flushing all the shorebirds—something I didn't want to do. If on the other hand, I elected to follow the end out to the beach, I stood a fair chance of finding the owner of the presumed kite. And, at 6:30 AM said owner(s) might not wish to be found.

My experience with kites has also led me to understand that an exertion of force upon a string will elicit a predictable (if not always favorable) response on the part of the associate kite. Put into the form of a hypothesis, this might read: *IF you tug on a kite string, THEN a kite will move.* Note that I did not say "fly." That is just one of the possible reactions (and based on my experience, it might be argued, the least likely).

I decided to test my hypothesis by giving the string one giant kid-sized tug. Benjamin Franklin would have been proud; Charlie Brown, envious. Like a phoenix on its five hundredth, a bright yellow kite burst out of the marsh, caught a strong, steady southwest wind, and rose straight up over South Cape May. Eureka!

Simultaneously, the Least Tern colony rose as a single bird to the attack, making a noise like a troop of scalded rats. Every blessed shorebird in the place threw on the afterburners and went to four winds. And there I was standing there flying this stupid kite.

Now, of course, for the purposes of this investigation, little need be done than qualify the original hypothesis to better align it with observed phenomena. The revision might read:

IF you pull a kite string, THEN a kite will move over an open marsh BUT every bird with an eye toward self-preservation will cut and run.

Which is all fine and dandy *except* it does not address itself to the fact that the anticipated reaction on the part of the birds was one that I would have preferred *not* to have happened. Had I given the matter a little thought I would have predicted the reaction and would not have tried pulling that string. I mean, the price, which was a blown birding trip, was not worth the knowledge gained—that kites are attached to strings and that birds are afraid of kites.

Sleeping shorebirds

Now, consider the similarity between my experience with the kite and these:

IF you apply organochlorine pesticides to large geographic areas, THEN you kill mosquitoes, which makes backyards safe for barbecues, BUT you decimate breeding populations of Peregrine Falcons and other raptors, because organochlorines cause egg shell thinning. Or. . .

IF you place Fish and Wildlife Service leg bands on Turkey Vultures, THEN you can trace their movements and learn about the migration of the species BUT excrement cakes on bands, cuts off circulation, causes gangrene, and only provides evidence to support the supposition that gangrene kills vultures.

Both of these well-intentioned actions had serious and unforeseen consequences, consequences of sufficient impact that, had they been foreseen, the initial actions probably would not have been taken. An ounce of prevention is worth a pound of cure. And here is another old saw worth considering. Sometimes the cure is worse than the cold. Consider the Peregrine Falcon dilemma and the attempts to set things right.

IF you grow Peregrines indoors, THEN you can put them back on the empty nest cliffs to re-establish the population. BUT you have to get rid of Great Horned Owls first because Great Horned Owls eat unparented young Peregrines at about $2,000 a sitting.

Well, then, how about this!

IF you put Peregrines out onto open salt marsh, THEN there will be no Great Horned Owls to eat them. BUT Peregrines that are introduced into coastal marshes eat (among other things) Least Terns—and Least Terns happen to be an endangered species in New Jersey.

No, I think it's about time that we spend just a little more effort assessing impact before the fact. All of man's actions affect the environment, well intentioned or not, and all too often the effects are only discovered later. I submit to any who might care to listen that *that environment is maintained best which is juggled least.*

There is a marvelous line out of Tolkien's *Lord of the Rings* that goes like this: "Even the wise cannot foresee all ends." And I, for my part, with the little wisdom allotted me, will think long and hard before I go pulling strings again.

Bookcase Bluebill

The bird sits on my parents' bookcase, incongruous beyond even my mother's far-reaching taste in decor. It's not that it doesn't go with the furniture or that it clashes with the color of the rug, but the bird stands apart, and a wandering eye will be drawn to it.

A birder would immediately identify it as a scaup and, if he were vain or imaginative enough, pin it down to species. He would also be wrong. To the man who carved it and to those who shot over it, it's a "stool," a "bluebill stool" (to be precise) —a decoy. It was a tool of the market-gunning trade, a vocation that flourished during the innocent, free-for-all time before conservation and died ironically of success. The gunners who plied their trade from the icy chop of Ironbound Island to the broad Susquehanna flats are gone along with the myth of inexhaustible numbers of waterfowl that were their mainstay. They left behind legends of the greatest waterfowling that the world will ever see and birds of native cedar who saw it all through eyes of brass.

The tale of decoys in America winds longer than the anchor lines that held them fast against the tide, and to speak of a decoy is to discuss a contrivance as wholly American as corn "likker." When the first European settlers stepped off the boat with blunderbuss in hand (and a taste for game sharpened by several weeks of salt port and hardtack) they found the locals (whose taste for game equaled their own) using decoys—of sorts. They weren't exactly "Harry Shourds" or "John Blairs," mind you. In fact, they were often little more than feather-stuck mounds of mud. But if these prototypes of the finely carved birds of the late Nineteenth Century would attract only the scorn of decoy collectors today, it should also be remembered that they did attract ducks.

The state of the art might have remained at this primitive level if not for several factors. First, the population along the Atlantic seaboard grew. As it did, so too did the demand for cheap and tasty fare or as this might otherwise be stated, a *market* developed. Second, the coastal hunter-farmer-fisherman who potted game to put food on the table discovered that there were greenbacks to be had in selling the surplus to the game-hungry seaboard cities. A man with enough skill could make a living by killing and selling game. He became a *supplier*. Finally, North American shorebirds and waterfowl, thousands and thousands of them, had long used the bays and marshes of the East Coast for migratory staging and wintering areas. This happy circumstance made them the obvious candidates for the title of *product*. In very short order, the hunting of migratory birds ceased to provide sport or sustenance. It became, instead, business.

Now, this whole happy partnership between market, supplier, and product hinged upon getting large numbers of birds out of the ozone and into the ice house. It was unlikely that ducks would go willingly, not without some firm persuasion. And during the long, long history of ducks and man, many different forms of persuasion have been used: nooses, snares, nets, impoundments, rocks, bolos, clay pellets shot from slings, stone-tipped projectiles loosed from bows, and so on. In frontier America, the most persuasive persuader rested on the pegs over the fireplace. Firearms, while not an American invention, have always been an American institution, and two hundred years ago they were about as indispensable as the automobile. Shooting ducks for the pot was already common practice and shooting birds on a grand scale, for market, required little more than upgrading a tried and proven system. It was only natural that, by and by, someone would remember the Indian and the feather-stuck dirt ball (you can't hide success). The decoy of the professional waterfowler emerged from the Indian's hunting genius and the need for permanence, durability and portability, a merger facilitated by a little Yankee ingenuity and some convenient stands of white cedar.

To a collector, the bookcase bluebill would be immediately recognized as a "Barnegat," a bird whose origin lies somewhere in the back-bay reaches of coastal New Jersey. Different regions developed different styles of carving, dictated by functional needs and constraints. A number of carving styles emerged up and down the Atlantic Coast so that now one may

Bluebill deke in the reeds

speak of a "Barnegat Black" or a "Cape May Black" or a "Long Island Black." And they might have very little in common—except for the fact that they were carved in the image and likeness of a Black Duck.

North along the rocky coast, the principal wintering birds are sea ducks: shoal duck, white-winged coot, black coot, skunkhead, whistler, and squealer (or, as a birder might know them today; eider, White-winged Scoter, Black Scoter, Surf Scoter, goldeneye, and Old-squaw). It isn't coincidence that the decoys that hail from Massachusetts north to Nova Scotia are of these species.

Birds of the northern coast were carved with a heavy hand from solid blocks of pine. They are characteristically oversized to increase their visibility, coarsely finished and blocky in design, and tough, to withstand rough water and rougher handling. The heads, as is the case with most decoys, were carved separately and later attached to the body. The well-fitted, inset joint that is the hallmark of northern birds bespeaks not only their origin but the arduous conditions that dictated the need for a durable, no-nonsense joint. Often birds were carved with bills agape and a mussel inserted between, a natural touch that observant professional waterfowlers noted and copied.

Long famous for its vast concentrations of wintering Canvasbacks, Redheads, and Canada Geese, the Chesapeake Bay is regarded by waterfowlers with something akin to reverence. The decoys that trace their origin to the many backwater reaches of the bay are largely of these three species.

Gunning with decoys on the Chesapeake was done with the aid of a diabolically efficient device, now outlawed, known as a sink box, a boat so weighted that its bulk remained below the waterline, concealing the gunner and betraying not even so much as the raised silhouette of a gunwale. Large, flat planes extended outward from the gunning box, preventing the craft from shipping water. Still, it was not a device to be used incautiously. A rising wind and a moderate chop could make a sink box as deadly for gunner as for quarry.

Large rafts of waterfowl are the rule in Chesapeake Bay, and gunners commonly used spreads of two- to five-hundred stool to make their set-ups appear natural and secure. The birds were carved from solid cedar or pine, broad of beam but with a fine sense of proportion and balance. Each was fitted with a lead keel weight, placed rearward, to provide ballast. This feature, more than any other, is the stamp of a Chesapeake decoy.

But the bookcase bluebill is a Barnegat, and if I confess to a certain amount of favoritism, I also submit that decoy carving reached its highest expression in New Jersey and Long Island waters. Unlike the blocky New Englanders and the broad-beamed Chesapeakes, Barnegat birds are slighter, slimmer, given to a modest exaggeration of some features, but clearly showing a concern for realism. One-man, one-boat gunning was the rule in Barnegat, and this custom dictated a key modification in decoy design. Several gunners might operate a gunning battery in Chesapeake and share the arduous task of transporting and spreading several hundred stool, but the sink box was never popular in New Jersey. Small, sleek shallow-draft cedar boats affectionately called "Barnegat sneak boxes," were favored by Jersey gunners and put a premium on the number of decoys a gunner could stow and, more importantly, on the weight of the birds.

Typical Barnegats have slight, well-proportioned bodies. The sometimes largish heads are artfully shaped and finely detailed to draw the attention of passing birds. The necks are short, more couched than extended, and there is nothing about their posture that betrays a hint of suspicion or unease.

The sneak's cargo problems inspired another refinement in the Barnegat carver's art. The body of the bird is a "dugout," halved and hollowed, its halves joined fore and aft with cedar dowels sanded flush and barely discernible. To the discriminating eye of a late-season "single" eyeing the gunner's rig, such a decoy would ride unconvincingly high in the water, so Barnegat birds, like Chesapeakes, are weighted. Unlike Chesapeakes with their keel weights, Barnegat birds are either fitted with inset weights or ballasted with flat, lead plates spiked to the underside with copper nails; both methods are concessions to the sneak's space limitations.

Two other carving styles have their roots in New Jersey waters, each as different from the Barnegat dugout as they are from each other. Birds of the Cape May region are similar in some respects to northern coast birds (and since more than a few Cape May families can trace their ancestry to Plymouth, perhaps the shared traits are more than coincidence). Cape May decoys are sometimes dugouts, sometimes not, and most seem to avoid the niceties of design that typify Barnegat or Delaware River birds.

To speak of a Cape May, one might just as well say "Black Duck," because hunting ducks in Cape May a century ago meant hunting blacks, just as it does today. Those who hunt Black Ducks hold the uncanny wariness of this bird in reverence bordering upon awe. A quarry that swerves at the sight of a carelessly tossed, spent shell makes the glint of sunlight on painted decoys an anathema to gunners. Cape May birds were commonly painted with flocked paint (mixed with dirt or fibers) to reduce reflected glare. And although Black Ducks still flared a hundred yards short of the decoys (just as they do today) at least it wasn't because of the paint.

The carving school that emerged along the Delaware River produced birds that were masterpieces of the carver's art, worked with a keen attention to detail and balance, Quaker-trim and aesthetically fine. Upriver birds are known for their raised, carved wings, and crouched heads. Pains were taken to make the birds as true to life as possible, because gunning, as it was conducted on the Delaware River, depended on ducks landing among the decoys. In theory, the more natural the decoy, the longer it took the new arrival to discover that it had fallen in with charlatans.

While the breasts of upriver birds are broad to prevent them from yawing unnaturally in the current, lower-river birds typically display extended and upturned breasts—a refinement ungainly in appearance but dictated by need. In the sluggish currents at the head of Delaware Bay, ice was commonly a problem. An upturned breast lifted a bird over slush and ice, and a bird lacking this feature would be pulled under by the force of drifting ice and the tug of the anchor line.

A hallmark of river birds is the skill with which they were painted, a testament not only to the attention given this aspect of the carver's art but also to the school's sweet-water heritage. It is unlikely that a school of carvers that placed such emphasis upon fine and detailed painting *could* have emerged except under conditions that offered some promise of permanence to their efforts. Whereas coastal decoys quickly become scarred and salt-blasted through constant immersion in salt water (requiring a total overhaul after a season's use), a river bird might need little more than a judicious touch of the brush. Masterpieces in any discipline are painted once, not annually.

There is a final level of distinction in decoys, one that goes beyond geography and has no equivalent in nature. Decoys are crafted by men sharing, perhaps, the same purpose but varying in terms of talent and know-how. Almost every coastal town had its carvers. Sometimes they were professional gunners, sometimes not, but only a Harry Shourds could carve a "Shourd's Brant." Only a Lee Dudley could produce a "Dudley Ruddy." The characteristic styles of these masters of the craft are as readily discernible as in any other art. Even though all carvers from Bay Head to Atlantic City carved Barnegat dugouts and followed established guidelines, the carvers still guided their drawknifes with styles as unique and traceable as fingerprints.

Decoy carvers did not ordinarily put their signatures on their birds, so identifying decoys today is largely deductive and often subjective. It sometimes happens, too, that heads crafted by one boat-house master would be affixed to bodies carved by another. Sometimes this was done by design, sometimes to repair a bird laid low by an inopportune pattern of No. 4 shot. For whatever reason, it sometimes makes for a troublesome mudiment of backwater accountability today.

The bookcase bluebill has all the earmarks of a Captain Jesse Birdsell of Barnegat Village—gunner, carver, legend. The bird's brow is high and exaggerated, and the back just behind the neck is deeply cleft. The tail is cropped in such a way that the upper surface resembles the narrowing keel of a boat. All of these traits say that the bird is a Jesse Birdsell.

What paint remains has suffered from sun, salt spray, hard use, and time. It suggests, rather than reveals, that the person who first guided a brush over it was an artist. This too says Birdsell. Where the paint has been scoured to bare wood, it can be seen that the bird is made of cedar, a token of its age. The stands of white cedar, coveted by early carvers, were all but logged out by the turn of the century. White pine succeeded it as the decoy maker's favorite.

The neck of the bookcase bluebill was broken close to the joint in some long unremembered accident, a malady common to decoys. It was repaired, broken again, repaired again, and several times overpainted. The leather tie that once secured the anchor line has long since rotted free. A copper brad replaced it.

When the bird is lifted and turned in examination, a dry metallic rattle comes from within, not unlike the sound that comes of shaking a long-rusting tin can. But cedar decoys don't rust, and the sound of wood chips on wood is neither dry nor metallic. Close scrutiny and an understanding of the nature of the beast resolves the riddle.

The bird, you see, is a decoy, and a short age ago, it rode with several score others in the winter sea of Barnegat. It is a spirit in league with gray, reluctant dawns, a falling tide, ice-sheathed oarlocks, wind-driven sleet, incoming birds, and the roar of Captain Birdsell's beloved double-barreled eight. There is nothing else on my parents' bookcase that can lay claim to such a heritage.

The proof of its past is hard bought. Patterned along its sides are a number of small, caulked holes, the badge of a bird that has more than once caught some of the shot intended for a flock putting into the decoys. The dry rattle is the sound of broken pieces of shot trapped, like memories, within.

No other item on my parents' bookcase can claim the distinction of having been shot, either. Although a few stray tokens to the hazards of the gunning trade enhance the appeal of the bluebill, an equal measure of shot in the flank of the Steuben vase would result in a rapid and irreparable depreciation of its net worth.

Whatever its present station in history, the bird is a decoy, a melded but unreconciled blend of artist's pride and cold purpose, a tension of opposites carved in wood. It is like hunting itself, a blend of opposing disciplines and emotions that somehow transcends contradiction. If that is not an easy thing to understand, it isn't through any failure of logic.

Many pieces of my parents' bookcase booty can boast great age or great value. Some are wrapped in memories greater than value. All but one ride in the calm of surrendered purpose, and some never had any purpose—except for sitting pretty.

The Birdsell bluebill rides on the tensions of its making and a purpose shelved but uncompromised, just as it once rode the chop off Barnegat Light. Given a fresh coat of paint, it could do so tomorrow.

First-Year Bird

The young Red-shouldered Hawk, a gray shadow moving silently through a world the color of wet ashes, flew out to the field's edge. She took a perch well below the tree line, lower than one that a Red-tailed Hawk might choose. If plumage didn't make it so obvious, the bird's choice of perches would have betrayed her lack of experience. An adult would have taken a perch that offered better protection from the rain.

If the bird remained still, there was nothing to show that she was not just another bark-stripped limb set against the backdrop of woodland. And the bird remained very still because she was very hungry. Her eyes were alive and occasionally her head moved in measured turns to study each hopeful movement in the leaves below.

She was a passage bird from New England, the only survivor of three nestlings. She had arrived three days ago, just before the weather closed in. For two days she had hunted without success. For two nights she had tried and failed to find a perch that offered protection from the rain and the icy touch of fog. But then, she was immature.

A week had passed since the bird had eaten her fill. Since then, a pair of cold-numbed frogs flushed from hibernation by storm-tide intrusion and a meadow vole with biorhythms at low ebb had been all. Poor fare. Yesterday, goaded by hunger, the bird had tried to feed on a road-killed skunk, but the passing cars intimidated her. When a curious driver stopped to watch, she left, not hungry enough, yet, to defend prey that was not her own from an adversary *that* formidable.

First-year bird

That would come later.

In the afternoon she had found this field and watched with hungry eyes the flock of cowbirds that flew off at her arrival but soon returned. Later still, she had watched a male Goshawk sprint from the trees, low and fast, overtaking the flock before it had gone forty feet. She left at dusk, still hungry. Now she was back.

The cowbird flock arrived ten minutes after the Red-shouldered took her perch.

To the right of where she waited, thirty head of cattle huddled in the protection of the trees, the steam rising from their bodies in the cold, windless air. Between the Red-shouldered Hawk and the cowbird flock were sixty yards of short-cut stubble, then a low area, too wet to plant, overgrown with goldenrod and milkweed. Ten feet beyond this weedy tangle was the near edge of the flock.

The weeds were the key. They would cover the 'shoulder's approach until she was almost upon the flock. Red-shouldereds are not sprinters. No Red-shouldered Hawk could hope to cross seventy yards of open field and capture something as quick and agile as a cowbird. Cover was everything.

But the flock was nervous. Maybe they recalled something of yesterday's Goshawk. Maybe they simply recognized the strategic weakness of their position. No doubt you develop a sense for such things when your life depends on it—and the birds that made up this flock could trace their ancestry back along lines of survivors, birds that had made the evolutionary cut when others did not.

Every few minutes, the flock would nervously take wing to light a few feet farther along. The timing was random. Several times the hawk had come within a shadow's breadth of making her move, checking herself just in time as the flock jumped.

The hunger that made all other concerns secondary spurred her to hurry.

She waited.

The knowledge that the flock might leave or that the Gos might beat her again put an edge to her concern.

She waited.

And as she waited she studied the birds in the flock and looked for injury or weakness or something that an eye could catch and hold when a flock explodes into motion. One adult cowbird was missing a foot but didn't seem hampered by it. Another younger bird had two broken flight feathers. Its movements were hampered, slower by a shade. The young cowbird seemed aware of its handicap and stayed well within the flock, avoiding the perimeter. But the Red-shouldered marked him anyway, carefully noting his position in relation to the other birds in the flock and the intervening patch of weeds. Cover was a two-edged sword. It would shield her attack—but for most of her approach, she would be unable to see her target. She would have one chance. It had to be right. It had to be precise. And it had to be blind.

The flock took wing, settled. Took wing, settled. The cattle began to get restless. Feeding time was drawing near. One old cow started off across the field toward the gate. The other filed behind. Their path would carry them between the hawk and the feeding cowbirds. Their movement would cover her own initial movement.

The hawk tensed, dropping her shoulders, leaning forward on the branch like a runner in the blocks. The lead cow passed ahead of the feeding flock; then the second, the third . . .

The flock took wing.

Settled.

The drop from the perch was done with no wasted motion, wings folded close to her body. Three feet off the ground, she leveled off, pumping now, picking up speed with each wing-beat, eyes fixed. She passed at hock-level behind the third cow in the string and in front of the nose of one startled calf. In eight more wing beats she covered the distance to the weeds, climbed slightly to clear the tops, still pumping. The flock, still twenty feet away, saw her instantly.

Speed and surprise were her allies. Before the flock could react, she had cut the distance to ten feet. By the time they were airborne, she was on them.

The hawk reached out for one bird in the tangle of wings, and closed her talons on empty air. Broken feathers appeared in front of her. The young Red-shouldered struck out with the other foot, braking with her wings and tail to keep from overshooting. Her foot closed over the bird—too slow. The cowbird twisted free, leaving nothing but feathers in locked talons.

The Red-shouldered Hawk sat momentarily amid the stubble, looked after the retreating flock, and surveyed the tribute of feathers in the closed fist of her talons. She returned to her perch, back turned to the field, and screamed her frustration to the universe.

The universe, predictably, was unmoved.

A truck piled high with silage pulled up to the gate. The Red-shouldered moved off, her cries lost in the mindless bawling of cattle impatient to be fed, her retreat covered by the maze of rain-glazed branches.

The Legend of Jesse Mew

"There he is," a nameless follower whispered hoarsely. A voice at the other end of the platform croaked, "It's him." All eyes turned to watch the dramatic entrance of the 1966 Dodge sedan, the car known as "White Trash." Fred Hamer, Official Hawk Counter at the Cape May hawk watch, brought up his binoculars like a salute to offer official confirmation.

"Yup, it's him all right." (There was no mistaking the awe in his voice.)

Trash moved stately as a queen in her court through the peak-season crush in the parking lot and turned lightly into a vacant spot that opened right in front of the hawk watch platform, just as if she knew it would be there.

Several of the hawk watch faithful nodded knowingly to each other. It was written: A WAY WOULD BE MADE FOR HIM IN CROWDED LOTS AND FAST FOOD DRIVE-IN WINDOWS.

The engine dieseled heavily for thirty seconds. Thin blue smoke hung like incense over the gutsy old heap and billowed uncaringly over the crowd standing open-mouthed and shoulder-to-shoulder on the platform. One or two asthmatics coughed irreverently.

Trash gave one final, thunderous belch of smoke, then shut down, making a noise like a Bessemer furnace giving breech birth to a Boeing 747. The hawk watch platform was enveloped in thick, oily fumes. The faithful, to a man, woman, and child, were brought to their knees by wracking coughs.

And when the smoke cleared, there he stood, the legendary

Jesse Mew—Professional Peregrine Watcher. Several of the faithful, their eyes streaming tears that ran rivulets down smog-blackened faces, nodded knowingly to each other. It was written: HIS MOVEMENTS ARE AS A CIVET CAT UNDER A NEW MOON—which was no small feat when you consider that removed of his Acme high-rise prairie stompers, Jesse stood six foot, seven and three-quarter inches.

Few, upon seeing the man for the first time, could describe him accurately—probably because to take in the whole unit at once would overload anything that approximated a normal functioning mind. And no individual seemed able to see Jesse the same way twice. This is particularly hard to understand, since Jesse never wore anything but the same crusty pair of Levi bellbottoms, a checkered shirt that looked as if it seconded as a dipstick rag, and a sun-bleached denim jacket that gave every appearance of having spent over half its life at the bottom of a bird cage.

His neck was long and sported a convulsively animated Adam's apple the size of a cue ball. His features were coyote sharp—the nose prominent, regal; the chin deeply notched. His hair was long, bleached white, and the consistency of spaghetti about thirty minutes overdone.

It went with the jacket.

Including guano, the whole unit weighed in at just over 109 pounds. Jesse Mew had the physique of a man just cut down from the cross.

But the color of his eyes was a matter of deep mystery and a subject of controversy. Jesse was never seen in public without his aviator sunglasses. Most believed that his eyes were deformed—the result of incalculable hours spent looking into the sun for towering Peregrines. One school said his eyes looked like twin hamburger patties, well larded; another said that they were a matched set of charcoal briquettes. But whatever their color, it was no secret that as organs of sight, they were remarkable. Jesse could read the Manhattan Telephone Directory White Pages at seventy paces.

His feats were clouded in myth and it might be that only half of what was attributed to him was true. It was believed that his

Peregrine in flight

father was a plastic injection mold technician specializing in geodesic dome interiors. His mother is nameless. Rumor has it that Jesse was born in the underground parking garage of an L.A. hospital. Admission was delayed because Mrs. Mew's Blue Cross/Blue Shield cards were not in hand for a polite but inflexible admissions nurse.

Little about Jesse's boyhood is known, but his grammar, spelling, and inability to figure outside of base three certified that he was the product of a public school education. Not until he reached the age of nineteen did there a emerge a story whose roots are verifiable. It seems that while the family was visiting relatives in Ithaca, New York, Jesse and his parents became separated. After long search, his father is said to have found him instructing a graduate seminar at the Laboratory of Ornithology on camber, aspect ratios, and wing-loading of North American falcons.

During his undergraduate years, Jesse bounced widely and often between universities—taking courses that he rarely completed, arguing with professors of ornithology, and having the unforgivable temerity to be right.

It was almost certain that during these early peregrinations he formulated his now-famous creed of "Natural Noninterference:"

"THAT ENVIRONMENT IS MAINTAINED BEST WHICH IS JUGGLED LEAST."

"If civilization," he would explain, "does some stupid and unwitting thing that blows a hole in the whole natural structure, anything done to try to right the situation will probably only make it worse."

Jesse particularly denounced that arcane backwash of the natural sciences known as: The School of Wildlife Management. "Why 'management'?" he would ask his followers. "Why not 'maintenance' or 'preservation' or 'wildlife, leave-it-the-hell-alone'? Who says that after two and a half billion years of working things out, a three-million-year-old hominid has the wherewithal to elbow his way onto the scene and do a better job?"

His teachings grew popular with the poor, the downtrodden—the undergraduates. The high nooky-nooks of academe grew jealous of his popularity and watched nervously as their course enrollment declined. Jesse was brought before a joint faculty/student board (packed with political science and home economics majors), denounced publicly on the trumped-up charge that his library card was overdrawn—and expelled.

Following this public humiliation, Jesse withdrew into the desert of the southwest, where he apprenticed himself to some half-cracked, Navajo medicine man turned falconer-and-bunco-artist who spent half his time bootlegging funny mushrooms and the other half trying to cross Peregrine Falcons with caracaras in the hope that he might interest the Arizona Highway Department in ordering wholesale lots of highly efficient roadkill remover that could be flown from the fist. It is whispered among raptor cultists at their gatherings in the back rooms of sandal shops and coffeehouses that the Indian could leave his mortal being and his spirit could fly free with Peregrines. Maybe it was true. Jesse believed it anyway.

Forty days later, Jesse was found face down in the Rio Grande by a seasonal park ranger leading a morning herp walk. He was naked, delirious, and barely alive when admitted to the hospital emergency room. The official park report reads "mugged and robbed." The doctor's diagnosis: "severe malnutrition, dehydration, and acute wind burn. Patient admitted in semi-conscious state, suffering delirium and under the apparent illusion that he could fly."

Recovery was slow. After a week, Jesse stopped trying to leap from eighth-floor windows but continued to sleep perched on the headboard and bated frantically whenever meals were served.

Following a two-year recovery in a nice quiet place out in the country, Jesse rocked the ornithological community by conducting a milestone study on autumn Peregrine migration by strapping himself to a jettisoned bale of hemp and dog-paddling around the Baltimore Canyon, one hundred miles east of Ocean City, Maryland, during September and October. The following year, he covered himself with plaster of Paris. Thus disguised as a three-hundred-year-old accumulation of whitewash, he staked out a nest ledge on the Coleville River of Alaska and observed the nesting strategy of tundra Peregrines from courtship to departure.

He returned next spring, but midway through the incubation, the tiercel disappeared. After a brief but decent interval, Jesse made known his intentions to the young widow, was accepted, and proved to be a good provider and capable father. At season's end, he and his new bride got off four strapping young pup Peregrines.

That was nine seasons ago. Each fall, filling in as a relief hawk counter at various hawk watches during peak-Peregrine period, Jesse made his way down the coast. During the winter he disappeared into the neotropics, but each spring he returned to his ledge overlooking the Coleville and to his lady. And now he was standing in the parking lot of Cape May Point State Park.

Jesse moved unhurriedly toward the trunk, rooted around through the mound of empties, and emerged with five cans of Skunkhead 10/40 motor oil. He unlatched the hood, inserted a magnum-sized funnel, and dumped all five cans into the crankcase simultaneously. Trash gurgled happily like a suckling child.

Having seen to the needs of his mount, Jesse made his way toward the platform. He took the steps two at a time and reached for Fred's extended hand.

"How you doing, Jesse?"

"Tolerable, Fred, tolerable. How 'bout yerself?"

"Just fine. How's the wife and kids? Everyone get off all right this year?"

"Got off without a hitch," Jesse answered proudly. "How's the flight been?"

"Oh, pretty fair," Fred pronounced. "How'd you like to count some Peregrines while I concentrate on other stuff?"

Jesse grinned widely, "Well, Ah guess Ah can do that. Ah guess Ah'd like that jes' fine."

Smiling shyly, Jesse moved through the press toward the other end of the platform. He stopped abruptly, brought his hand up to block the morning sun, and announced casually, "Peregrine coming in."

A blue-backed bird arched over the trees, threw on the afterburners, and burned a hole through the early morning haze hanging over the marsh. A paunchy, balding man wearing Italian climbing boots, a string tie, and an Abercrombie-and-Fitch safari jacket bedecked with no fewer than sixty bird club patches elbowed his way to Jesse's side. In a voice heard from one end of the platform to the other he announced, "Peregrine, all right. Second after hatching year immature female I make it; subspecies *borealis*." He turned with staged familiarity, gazed (one expert to another) at the figure towering three heads above him, and dug himself in just a little bit deeper. "Not much question about that one."

Jesse gazed mildly at the upturned face for a pensive few seconds and replied, "Her name's Albert." Jesse whistled shrilly and hailed, "Yo, Albert, you old plover-eater, you."

Albert altered his course forty degrees to pass directly over the platform, executed a neat little wing dip, and climbed steadily as he moved out over Delaware Bay.

The "expert" pulled his head down between his shoulders and moved, quickly, toward the exit ramp. Several of the faithful nodded knowingly to each other. It was written: THE CHARLATANS SHALL TRIP OVER THEIR OWN WORDS AND ALL MUMMERY BE LAID BARE IN HIS PRESENCE.

"That a friend of yours, Jesse?" Fred inquired.

"Neighbor," said Jesse. "Two bluffs up."

Jesse, completing his shift to the south side of the platform, was heedless of the friends, followers, and admirers who stared in unabashed veneration; the few bolder ones reached out to touch the hem of his bellbottoms. From his daypack, Jesse pulled a pair of beat-up Hensolt binoculars (which he was never seen to use), a rebuilt stainless-steel hand counter, and two sixpacks of Dr. Pepper. Jesse was a Pepper addict.

Life on the platform returned to a semblance of normalcy. Fred clicked off sharpies and kestrels on the north side; Jesse pulled Peregrines out of the ozone on the right. He averaged fifteen to twenty an hour.

Occasionally, Jesse turned his head sideways, Adam's apple abob, peered upward into what looked for all the world like empty sky, and made a notation on his data form. Seeing the puzzled looks around him, Jesse smiled and explained.

"Stealth Peregrines—flying beyond the limit of conjecture. That'd be a code-eight bird on the data sheets (if they went up that high). It *is* kinda tough picking 'em up on a day like this," he added generously. "Lots of heat inversions—blocks reception."

As he was taking the three o'clock weather readings, Jesse's face turned pale and he grasped the rail as if for support. Almost immediately, a young hawkwatcher called out, "Peregrine! Peregrine coming in three fields over Cape May." The masses gasped, thunderstruck, the foundation of their faith rocked. Jesse Mew beat to a call by a total unknown! Such a thing had never happened in memory.

Fred, his face the picture of concern, looked down the length of the platform and inquired anxiously, "Jesse, you O.K.?"

Jesse smiled weakly and shook his head in affirmation. With an effort he said, "Yeah, no problem, jes' a little dizzy is all." And then turning to the young hawkwatcher, he said apologetically, "It's not a wild Peregrine, I'm afraid. It's a Pseudogrine, *Falco pseudogrinus*. It's one of them test-tube birds with the garbled bloodlines; the ones they used to grow indoors back in the DDT-panic when the sensible thing would have been jes' to let the birds go an re-establish themselves naturally. Folks jes' don't seem to have no faith in nature workin' things out herself—and less patience. It do beat all."

"Oh," the youngster said (more relieved than hurt). "But how could you tell it wasn't a real bird?"

"Ah felt a weakening in the force," Jesse allowed.

Several of the faithful nodded knowingly to each other. It was written: THOU SHALT HAVE NO ERSATZ PEREGRINES BEFORE THEE.

The flight dwindled as the afternoon wore on. The shadow of the lighthouse reached slowly but inexorably for the hawk watch platform. The faithful, singly or in small groups, departed. Most would be late for wherever it was they were going.

On the empty platform, Fred closed the space separating himself and Jesse. They both stood for a time saying nothing, savoring the deepening evening. Words weren't necessary. Indeed, sometimes words impede communication.

Fred finally broke the silence.

"So how long you planning on staying, Jesse?"

"Contract with that pirate at the Observatory runs to the fifteenth but Ah may stay on a few more days if the flight looks good—and he knows it, too. But Ah got to git goin' by the twentieth at the latest. Ah got a ways to go, yet."

"I guess so," Fred said. "Well, I'm calling it a day; flight seems to have died. You going to watch for a bit?"

"Yea, Ah guess Ah'll hang on 'n keep an eye on things for a bit. Ah got me some friends that like to travel at night. Less traffic, they insist, and it's easier on the eyes."

With this, Jesse reached up and casually removed his shades. Fred was one of the handful of people on earth who *knew* what color Jesse's eyes were. And although Fred noted that the effect wasn't as startling as the first time, it was still hard to feel comfortable looking into eyes that drew all the shapes and colors of the world into themselves and reflected nothing but mystery in return. It was a gaze that was both benign and piercing, and he could never decide, somehow, whether the eyes seemed shallow, like standing water on an asphalt highway, or like two holes cut through the dark universe where depth has no meaning.

They might have been blue once. But maybe the medicine man wasn't so cracked after all.

Birdathon '83—A Saab Story

The road is visible in snatches: smeared impressions of a highway at the wave of a windshield wiper. Each sweep of the blade grants a moment of safety interspaced by leaps of blind faith.

. . . here's the road . . . here's the road . . . here's the road . . .

It's like a game. Connect the points with a line that gets you (safely) from here to there. Just for realism, just to keep the adrenalin flowing, every once in a while the image alters.

. . . here's a car . . . here's the median . . . here's a tree . . . HERE'S A . . .

But my reactions to these challenges are mechanical and indifferent. Fatigue has robbed the game of any pleasure now.

Couched in soggy velour, wrapped in resignation and the passenger seat, is *American Birds'* Regional Editor Bill Boyle. Visible in the rear view mirror: Pete Bacinski, the J.J. Audubon of Lyndhurst, New Jersey, and David Sibley, the hottest thing to hit birding since the Phoenicians melted sand. Beneath us is a Saab 900 Turbo. Behind us, the 1983 Birdathon.

When did this story begin?

I don't know. Lots of times. Lots of places. Last night, at midnight (to be strictly accurate), just twenty hours ago. Or last week on the "dry run." Or last year when we blew the doors off the old New Jersey Big Day record of 171 species, weighed in with a total of 185, and planted the conviction that two hundred species in twenty-four hours was possible outside of Texas or California . . .

. . . Or maybe in 1979 when Pete B. and I ran our first Big Day together . . . or when I was four and first lifted my father's

*6 x 20 Zeiss binoculars from his desk drawer and felt the
magic in them . . . or when Peterson codified the law . . . when
Ludlow Griscom broke with the shotgun school . . . when the
first gunslinger notched his six-shooter . . . on the sixth day
when God made birders . . . or the fifth, when he made the
birds of the air . . .*
   . . . points on a line . . . points on a line . . . points on a line . . .

   *The Saab moves surely down the rain-sheathed highway;
fifteen-inch Pirelli radials knife through standing water to find
firm footing beneath. The car moves with a responsiveness
that is a step above control. And there is just a hint of impatience; a pouting eagerness because the driver won't let her
run.*

Bird in the bush

We had mapped out our assault at a strategy session in March. If they ever establish a Birders' Hall of Fame, they can call this meeting the Sandy Hook Summit.

They can call it anything they wish.

Finding two hundred species was going to take more than skill and luck. It was going to take planning. There are, in New Jersey during the second week in May, about 190 species of birds that are front-line possibilities for a Big Day—although, admittedly, some like Pied-billed Grebe and Wild Turkey are tucked into out-of-the-way nooks and crannies of the state and, given the time factor, become untenable candidates for a working hit list.

There are another forty or so birds that fall into a category marked "present but not certain to be seen." On the reasonable end of the scale, these include birds like American Bittern and Alder Flycatcher—birds that, because of weather conditions or timing, might be missed. On the distal end of the scale are birds such as Curlew Sandpiper—birds that are just few and far between. Beyond these two hundred and thirty possible species is a vast and not-to-be-seriously-considered mass of possibilities labeled "dreams."

In the broadest sense of "strategy," we would have to do three things in order to reach two hundred species: time our assault for the optimal overlap between wintering and breeding species; plot a route, cut bare of wasted time, that would intercept all key habitats and the birds that they hold; and tie down in advance as many borderline species as possible.

The mechanics for achieving these three broad goals were not manifest. Consensus did not come easy.

All of us agreed quickly that Saturday, May 21, was too late. The wintering birds would be gone. We opted, instead, for a May 14 run with a second assault planned for May 21 (just in case). We dismantled our record-setting route of 1982 and rebuilt it from scratch by ruthlessly cutting unproductive or redundant sites, adding locations of greater promise, and plotting a course that was mindful of every conceivable contingency—traffic, tides, gas stops, coffee shop locations. We subjected everything to merciless down-to-the-minute scheduling and still, somehow, managed to buy one hour of undesignated time: a buffer against crisis, a coin to cash in on a windfall condition (a warbler fall-out, bonus shorebirds) or to use to track down misses at the end of the day.

No, consensus did not come easily. Pete Bacinski howled at the prospect of cutting Bull's Island (home of the Cliff Swallow) from the itinerary. Bill Boyle lobbied hard to include a grass-land species site "that wasn't too far off the route," and I dug in my heels at the prospect of a fall-back dicky-bird stop at Princeton.

Everyone had a site that was too dear to drop; everyone had another that he deemed too unproductive for the price. But when it was over, we were sure we had a winner. Two hundred species was going to be close, real close. And we even adopted a name for the ad hoc combatants: THE GUERRILLA BIRDING TEAM; and a motto: HIT AND RUN.

What we needed was a car—and not just any car, either. What we needed was a car that could meet some pretty tough and unusual demands.

It had to be fast enough to melt the white line on an inter-state and tough enough to gouge its way along a pine barrens goat path like a peccary in heat. It would have to handle like a New York City taxi with the promise of a fifty dollar tip in the driver's ear and be able to go from flat out to flat zero in less time than it takes to say, "Hey what's that bird sitting on the wire?

It would have to be engineered for comfort (to offset the effects of twenty-four hours in the saddle), provide excellent visibility in 360 degrees (plus a sunroof), and offer ample trunk space for scopes and tripods, with four doors that opened W I D E for fast exits and quick re-entry. On top of this, it had to be mechanically dependable to the point that malfunc-tion was a consideration to leave behind. And it had to be safe, because when safety is a question, concentration is under-mined.

In other words, what we wanted was the ultimate birding car.

After sifting all of the domestics and imports through the

fine mesh of established need and fifteen years of piston worship, we found there was really only one top contender for a Birdathon staff car. But would Saab-Scania of North America be willing to lend us one for the assault?

The instruments on the dash stand out in sharp relief against a world washed clean of color. Twin headlights, probing for danger, lance into the gloom. Unable to resist the temptation, I feather the accelerator lightly and watch three needles begin to climb: the turbo gauge and tach quickly, eagerly; the speedometer, steadily. I ease back and the engine sighs in protest.

Ground fog lay heavy over the remains of glacial Lake Passaic dying, now, these ten thousand years. Barred Owls screamed their visions. The world, poised between the death of one day and the birth of another, seemed to consider them. The world always does.

Saab 900 . . . birdathon staff car

We rolled to a halt on the old dike road. Four doors opened as if moved by a single hand. A dark figure emerged from each and strode quickly to form the points of a ritual square. Heads bowed, we waited.

One by one the night birds betrayed themselves. One by one we chanted their names aloud—Virginia Rail, Sora, Common Moorhen, American Woodcock. Somewhere a Screech Owl chuckled softly. Somewhere a Least Bittern and an American Bittern did not, and would not for all the cues and promptings that poured from Bill Boyle's cassette. If they laughed at us, they did it silently (because even the laugh of a bittern is known to Sibley and Boyle).

"Time," said Bill. Without protest we left the dike behind. The Great Swamp was Bill's fief. For four weeks he had stalked its pools and hardwood glades as he staked out birds on his assigned hit list. If he couldn't find them, they weren't to be had.

A shadow of a bird flashed through the headlights. "Solitary Sandpiper," said three voices; "Spotty," said one. Without prompting or discussion each of us traced back along lines of thinking that led to our individual identifications, searching for a flaw. "You're right," the lone dissenter proclaimed quickly. "Solitary. I thought it was smaller at first."

Bill guided us to a stop. "Great Horned Owl nest over in the trees with two young in it," he explained as he rolled down the window. He need not have bothered, not with the window or the identification. The impatient screams of hungry owl pups made even the night uneasy.

We left the swamp at 1:30, right on schedule, with six birds on the "must get" list in the bag, but with both bitterns unaccounted for. It was twenty minutes to Troy Meadows—automatic back-up site for freshwater nocturnals.

We jumped the chain-link fence in commando fashion and navigated the narrow catwalk leading out into the marsh on the balls of our feet. It is an old walkway, repaired at intervals by the power company but always at a pace several steps behind need. The skeletal frames of high-tension towers loomed overhead. The air crackled with their malevolence.

Troy surrendered nothing to our list. The catwalk and the

hope that lured us farther and farther out into the marsh cheated us. Bitterns were as silent as the shadows cast by stones.

This car is a product of evolution; it fills an asphalt niche. It is not a racing car. It is not a living room on wheels. It is a creature that sees asphalt ahead an affront and highway behind a delight—a creature in perfect tune with its environment.

West on Route 80 now, the road that spans the continent. Racing against dawn to Allamuchy Mountain, we hoped to add Wild Turkey to the list with a fast throw of the dice. Gravel flew in our wake as we pulled up under the shadows of sugar maples. Night-sharpened senses brought the acid bite of dairy cattle to our noses and the chilling call of a distant rooster to our ears. Bill hit the tape and the ersatz gobbler stirred to life, volume FULL . . .

". . . GOBBLEOBLOBLOBLOBLOBL . . . OBLOBLOBLOBL-OBL . . . OBLOBLOBLOBLOBL . . . "

A station wagon roared up the road, stopped, disgorged two serious-looking camouflage-clad men who each grabbed equally serious-looking autoload shotguns. They gazed quizzically at us and then charged up the hill. Weighing the implications of this new turn of events, we deemed it wise to leave quickly.

The Saab careened into the parking area near the old elevated road-bed at Waterloo with only the mildest application of brakes. Catapulted from the car, we marched doubletime up the tracks overlooking the river. All signs of fatigue were gone now. Put in a blender, separated in a centrifuge, we could have provided enough adrenalin to make a dead brontosaurus backstroke across Saskatchewan. This was the magic hour before dawn on the day that transforms everything avian into treasure.

Every bird is a prize on a Birdathon. All birds count as one, no matter how common or how rare; a cowbird rates as high as a Bachman's Warbler. And if the hour that bonds the day to the night is one filled with treasure, Waterloo is the mother lode.

One by one we gathered them: cardinal, towhee, Wood Thrush, phoebe, catbird, and robin. Mixed in with the amethysts and garnets were emeralds and rubies, the ones that might have been missed—kingfisher, Ruffed Grouse, Solitary Vireo, Purple Finch, and a pearl of great price, a windfall extra—Olive-sided Flycatcher.

And just before leaving, David did it again—second year in a row, a pick-up-from-behind Black-billed Cuckoo that tried to sneak across the road when our backs were turned. It was 6:30. We were behind schedule.

Allamuchy Boy Scout Camp is one of those clutch, hole-card stops. It is a place to get those make-or-break species, the borderline expecteds, and a place to intercept first-run misses. In ten minutes, we picked up both waterthrushes, Brown Creeper, and Cerulean Warbler and plugged a few ominous holes in our passerine list.

With both scheduled upland songbird sites in the rearview mirror, Pete did a count and came up with ninety-one—two birds ahead of 1982's record-setting run. So far, so good.

A collie, worn out by years of affection, regards the world from her favorite spot under the juniper, next to the house on Beekman's Lane. She watches a car pursued by a tremendous dust cloud come down the road. The car unexpectedly stops. She raises her head and watches as four doors spring open and a person emerges from each. One gestures wildly at a small, short-tailed sparrow sitting on a fence. Another tries to draw the others' attentions to two scrawny, bug-eyed, chicken-like birds stalking a plowed field. The third points and shouts in the direction of a low cruising, white-assed hawk, and a fourth appears to go into a seizure over some nondescript, flat-headed bird singing in the grass. The collie sighs and drops muzzle to paws.

"People are crazy."

The thought is not a new one to her.

After quick but heated debate we opt to bypass Bull's Island and shoot south, making a quick stop at Princeton. The decision means that we forfeit Cliff Swallow—but we buy a precious hour and a half. One sure bird is not worth that high a price.

Institute Woods, Princeton, is saturated with birders hot on the trail of peak-week warblers. We pick up Warbling Vireo, shift Black-throated Green and Nashville Warblers from the lost to the found column, and escape without losing too much time in exchanges of information with friends and fellow birders.

Assunpink Fish and Gamelands surrenders Blue Grosbeak, Northern Bobwhite, and Orchard Oriole without a struggle. The lake yields a lingering Common Loon, and Turkey Vultures dot the horizon.

This marks the halfway point on the itinerary. We stare at our watches and look at each other in disbelief. It's only 10:30. Ahead lie seventy miles of sterile sand and stunted pines called, appropriately, the barrens. For birding purposes, its sole advantage seems to be that the roads are straight, uncluttered by traffic, and lightly patrolled. With little to do but wait, everyone relaxes.

Bill nudges me gently, gestures toward the back seat, and wryly suggests that I avoid bumps. In the mirror, Pete Bacinski snores peacefully. I smile and convey my understanding to Bill with a nod. He shakes his head, "no," and gestures to Pete's left. An adjustment of the mirror brings into focus the horror of a hand pouring a stream of viscous amber onto a heavily peanut-buttered slab of bread lying face-up on the seat. I shudder and center my attention on the road. Does honey come out of velour?

What kind of an animal is this car most like? It isn't a wolf. There are lots of wolves on the highway. It isn't like the hulking buffaloes that come from Detroit. It's not one of the stiffly pouncing foxes of England or the scurrying ferrets of Japan, or the baronial badgers of Germany. No, it is not like these.

It is a like a cat, I think. Its leanness masks an underlying power. Its movements are fluid and quick without effort. It seems always crouched to spring. Even when it stands, there is motion.

But it should be a fish today, in this rain, on this river of asphalt. Not a shark—except maybe a Mako. It is not stupid like a marlin or vicious like a blue. No, there is intelligence in this car. Maybe it would be a dolphin then? I don't know. I don't know fish very well. (I don't know fish at all if I think a dolphin is a fish. Just drive and leave the fish alone.)

A detour on Route X directs us through a rabbit warren of cottage communities. We emerge onto Route 70 not far from Lebanon State Forest. We decide to drop in for its cluster of semi-tough species (Contingency Plan Seven-B). The sidetrip is good for Summer Tanager and Eastern Bluebird, but Red-headed Woodpeckers elude us. After a decent interval (about thirty or forty seconds), we move out.

Hit and run.

Brigantine National Wildlife Refuge is a "must stop" on any Big Day circuit. No place offers easier access to more salt marsh species. We hit the dikes at the crack of noon, round them in the allotted one-hour limit, and encounter difficulty only once—a near mutiny when a Curlew Sandpiper in breeding plumage plops down in front of us; David has to be dragged back to the car. Brig was a treasure trove. Along with the must-gets like Gull-billed Tern and White-rumped Sandpiper, we garnered both teal, lingering shovelers, a Ruddy Duck, a Merlin, and another gift—American Avocet.

Pete checked the list on the exit road. And then he checked it again. The count stood at 171! The time said 1:15 PM. Last year's count at this point was 158. Thirteen birds ahead of last year and almost one hour ahead of schedule. Incredible.

The back side of the Stone Harbor heronry offered a quick eyeball-to-eyeball confrontation with a Yellow-crowned Night-heron. Great Channel produced a small flock of Red-breasted Merganser. Higbee Beach yielded a chat (but not without a fight), and Pete B. came through with a clutch save on a near-miss—a late, soaring Broad-winged Hawk.

The South Cape May Meadows was good for Piping Plover, Purple Sandpiper, Black Scoter, and Pectoral Sandpiper (a gift). We skipped Cape May Point. It had nothing left to offer us.

Now it was our turn, David's and mine. From here on it was a mop-up operation—a point-to-point search for birds missed and for birds tied down. A search of the list showed that we still needed (incredibly!) Killdeer and (not unexpectedly) Horned Lark. The Cape May County Airport was the third and second line of defense for each, respectively—and it was, too.

Cape May County Park gave us the Red-headed Woodpecker we had missed at Lebanon State Forest (but not the Red-bellied Woodpecker that was supposed to be there). The Yellow-throated Warbler couldn't be coaxed into calling, and Moore's Beach Road grudgingly surrendered a Prothonotary Warbler and a Hairy Woodpecker (second fall-back sites for both species)—but again, no Red-bellied Woodpecker.

Out on the marsh, luck surrendered the Least Bittern that fate had cheated us out of eighteen hours earlier, and it traded us a Reeve for the Lesser Yellowlegs that should have met us there.

Pete did it again. A distant speck became an immature Bald Eagle under Questar-assisted judgement. And just before leaving, a raptor flashed overhead whose manner and movement shouted "PEREGRINE"—number 186—a new state record!!!

During the ensuing period of wholesale congratulations, David coolly watched the bird's progress and painfully announced, "It landed on a new Peregrine hack tower out in the marsh."

Pete scratched the bird from the list.*

It was a shaken foursome that headed for Turkey Point. To have lost the record in such a fashion shocked our resolve. When the Kentucky Warbler couldn't be coaxed into song at our one and only Kentucky site, it sent spirits plummeting. Our goal of two hundred species was slipping from our grasp.

A shoestring Lesser Yellowlegs at the Maurice River Bridge

*According to the standards established by the American Ornithologists Union, an introduced species must breed for ten years in order to be regarded as an established species. Peregrine Falcons, extirpated in New Jersey, were artificially reintroduced in 1976 and therefore could not be counted.

gave us back the record. Dividing Creek produced Yellow-throated Warbler, Acadian Flycatcher, Hooded Warbler, and finally, a Red-bellied Woodpecker at our fourth and final fall-back location.

Dusk found us overlooking the marshes of Delaware Bay. King Rails sounded off all around us. In the distance, a Whip-poor-will called, then a Chuck. The count stood at 194. We could still go to Marmora for Black Rail or Greenwich for Common Barn Owl—or we could pack it in and try for 200 next week.

We packed it in.

An angry battlezone of flashing brakelights blocks the highway. Somewhere ahead someone is driving at a crawl and another driver, intimidated by conditions, keeps back, blocking the passing lane. Other cars pack in behind, tight as sheep in a chute—a stupid, dangerous situation, an accident just waiting to happen.

The toll booth at mile seventeen looms ahead. Two exact-change lanes are open; there is one booth with an operator. In a culture groomed to believe that machines do everything quicker and better, the whole angry, impatient pack stampedes for the exact-change lanes. The Saab cuts inside, unchallenged, window open, hand out, quarter gleaming. The attendant extends his arm, palm open for a fast transfer.

Two arms of torque warp themselves around our middles, pulling us back in our seats, and the throaty whine of the turbo rises in our ears. The road ahead is an open ribbon of gray as the Saab pulls away from the toll booth. Other cars close in behind, sealing the back door.

Today, March 21, never really had a chance. The Great Swamp rumbled with thunder under a sky that was dressed for a funeral. Off and on, there was rain. Each site couldn't help but be measured against last week's effort—and each site seemed to come up shorthanded or to break even only at a greater expenditure of time and effort.

There was no Olive-sided Flycatcher at Waterloo. The Solitary Sandpipers were gone, Purple Finch with them. The Brown Creepers at Allamuchy were nowhere to be found. And though birds were found that were missed on the May 14 run—Willow Flycatcher, Bay-breasted and Mourning Warblers—the register rang up net loss at each site. When we left Brigantine Refuge with 159 species in the bag, we were twelve birds shy and an hour and a half behind the May 14 run.

And then it started to rain.

And then it started to pour.

At 6:00 PM, we pulled into the parking area at Jakes Landing, wet, tired, and looking for harrier. In the last three hours we had added exactly four birds to the list and four hundred pounds of mud and rainwater to the interior of the car. When it became clear after a ten-minute vigil that even harriers wouldn't fly in weather like this, a voice vote was taken.

When did this story begin? I really couldn't say. But I know when it ended. It ended thirty minutes ago, at Jakes. Two hundred species were not going to happen in 1983. We would have to settle for last week's 194—a New Jersey record, but six birds shy of our mark.

Epilogue

For once the beer at the C-View tastes flat. The cheese-steak hoagies are stringy. The chef skimped on the fried onions. The peppers have no bite.

Two tables over, a young couple argues bitterly and loudly about borrowing money from parents. Next door, a whiney two-year-old annoints his sailor suit with a full bowl of Manhattan clam chowder and starts to scream. At the bar, four girls touting haircuts that look like someone planned on finishing them another time stop trying to catch our eyes and turn their sights on easier game. Nobody takes any notice. There isn't enough combined enthusiasm in the four of us to fall asleep.

Suddenly, David stops staring a hole in his mug and looks past us, toward the window. His eyes, twin pinpoints of light, brighten with awareness. Bill Boyle turns, gazes thoughtfully at the glassy unpocked puddles lying deep in the street, downs his mug, and smiles secretly. Pete Bacinski, stopped in mid-bite, studies the light creeping across the table in front of him. Chuckling softly, he finishes the end piece and plants both feet firmly on the floor and both hands palms down on the table.

Four pairs of eyes meeting across the table carry a single thought.

Sherry, a waitress worn out by hours of rainy-day patrons, regards her bill pad from her favorite spot at midbar. She hears a loud commotion from the corner table and raises her head to find several piles of scattered bills, four pushed-back chairs (two of them still in motion), and a group of indeterminable size going through the exit door. She sighs and drops her face to her pad.

"Birders are crazy."

The thought is not a new one to her.

On the curb, the tawny-colored Saab waits, patient as a cat. Even while standing, it seems to be in motion.

A Lifer for Roger

The thought brought me up short. *"You don't suppose she meant the field on the other side of the house?"*

It didn't seem likely. Linda's instructions had been simple and direct: the bird is in the field across the street from the house with the blue whale in the back yard (which really narrows down the options). And we *had* searched that field, not twenty minutes ago, turning up one Eastern Kingbird, two species of swallow—but no Fork-tailed Flycatcher.

But, "across the street from the house with the blue whale" is not as interpretation-free as you might think. I'm a product of suburbia, born and raised in one of the planned labyrinths that popped up in the post-war era. *Across the street* to the suburbanized mind invariably means: across the street from the *front* of the house (which is the only across the street a suburban kid ever knows). There are next-door neighbors, back-yard neighbors, but only one *across-the-street neighbor*.

Farm houses, of course, are different, particularly farm houses that sit on corners—like this one did. A farm house that sits on a corner has, potentially, two fields that might be construed to be "across the street".

But, I still didn't give this alternate street theory much credence. The bird, quite simply, had disappeared overnight. A Fork-tailed Flycatcher hadn't lingered in Cape May since Otway Brown had run into this tine-tailed tropical waif back in 1939. It was gone.

But being only one member of a five-member team didn't

give me the right to leap to any unilateral decisions. I felt duty-bound to throw the possibility out to the floor.

"You know," I said, "we didn't check the field *next* to the house with the blue whale."

Everybody stopped. Nobody said a word.

"It's probably not worth going back for," I added. "We're thirty minutes behind schedule as it is."

"Oh, come on," Pete Bacinski lobbied. "It's not *that* far out of the way."

"We could just go up Bayshore Road on the way out," Bill Boyle suggested. "Just a quick stop."

"I think it's worth trying," David Sibley added.

I turned to meet the gaze of the fifth member of our Big Day birding team, a man whose face would be recognized instantly in any birding spot in North America—a man whom I have known nearly all my life but met for the first time barely twenty-four hours ago.

"Yes, let's give it a try," said Roger Tory Peterson.

All my life doesn't seem like a very long time, now, but it would have seemed interminably long to the scrawny kid who used to wait anxiously next to the mail box on Roosevelt Avenue in Whippany, New Jersey. No zip code. They didn't have zip codes back then.

He was waiting for the red, white, and blue mail truck that was moving down the street, methodically stopping at each yard like a hummingbird going down a row of flowers. He was waiting for the manila envelope with the bold blue label that read—FROM NATIONAL AUDUBON SOCIETY: FOR PETER J. DUNNE. Inside were leaflets, Junior Audubon Society leaflets all about different birds. They were ten cents each—if you ordered six, they were only five cents each. But even five cents each was tough on a budget of thirty-five cents a month and it had taken a long time to get all the leaflets he had wanted.

He had gotten the one about the Baltimore Oriole (State Bird of Maryland), Leaflet No. 26, first along with the Red-winged Blackbird (Leaflet No. 25) because it was common in the tussock-grass marshes near his parents' house (and because it

Fork-tailed Flycatcher

was one of the first birds he had identified). He had added Barn Swallow (Leaflet No. 32), Yellow Warbler (No. 139), and Indigo Bunting (No. 27). He'd never seen an Indigo Bunting (the bird was simply too beautiful to ever see), but he had gotten the leaflet anyway—just in case.

Each leaflet contained a color plate (that he called a picture) and a matching line drawing (to color in). And he read those leaflets, and read them and read them—until there wasn't any need to anymore, because he had memorized them. They were written by a man named Roger T. Peterson.

When the boy was twelve, he received a marvelous gift—a two-volume book about birds published by the National Geographic Society. Inside the book about *Song and Garden Birds* was an essay by Roger Peterson entitled "What Bird is That?". It described the Peterson System for identifying birds. There were eight questions to ask when you wanted to identify a bird—and the boy memorized them, too.

These were the books he used as his field guides. They used lots of photos. So, it's not surprising that for several years Hermit Warblers were regular spring migrants through Whippany and waterthrushes went unidentified. New Jersey wasn't exactly what you would call "Northern" but it was *still* a long way from Louisiana. He didn't know any other birders so he didn't find out about *real* field guides until some years later (in fact, until after he'd worked the waterthrush problem out). And, know what? The field guide was written by his old friend and mentor, Roger Peterson.

But even that is a long time ago, now; a distant point on a road that carried a suburban kid with an interest in birds to Cape May, New Jersey. And all along the route, there was a man named Peterson. A man who had helped and guided millions of young minds (just like his). The man who taught first one generation, then another, and another the skills they needed to learn about and enjoy the world they found around them—Roger Tory Peterson.

These were some of the thoughts that skittered across my mind one day last January when I called Dr. Peterson at his home. An idea was developing, an exciting idea. We were

71

thinking about modifying the big day birding tradition and birdathon concept to incorporate an element of competition—*team* competition. On May 19, 1984, big day birding teams representing birding clubs and organizations from several states would bird New Jersey, using all of their knowledge and skills to locate as many birds as possible. There was much to commend the idea. But, there were uncertainties, too. And it would be unthinkable to contemplate an event that would carry birding onto uncharted ground without soliciting the wisdom of the Grand Master of North American Birding. How would he regard the idea? Would he favor it? I needn't have worried.

"It's the next logical step," he said with a conviction that would have put even the most doubtful mind at ease. "Did you know," he continued, "that the British have been holding a two-team competition for several years, now. I've just written an introduction to a book about it called *The Big Bird Race*," he continued, infectiously enthusiastic. "I'll send you a copy. You'll probably want to read it . . ."

And then he said something that sent my mind tumbling end over end.

"Whose team can I be on? Can I be on yours? We should start at Troy Meadows, don't you think? And then move on toward Boonton for passerines at dawn . . . "

This, in case you are not a birder, is a little like having the Pope ask whether he can go to church with you on Sunday.

". . . *Let's give it a try,*" said Roger Tory Peterson, the man with the fine spun frosting of hair that frames two of the bluest, kindest eyes ever to regard the world. And he said it with good reason.

For one thing, our tally stood at 183 with only two hours of daylight left. There were only eighteen species of birds that we felt that we still had a shot at gathering between now and midnight. Several of these could be counted on to fail. It was going to take a little luck and a couple of unexpected sightings if we were going to reach our goal of two hundred species in twenty-four hours. We were *so* close—and Fork-tailed Flycatcher was *not* accounted in those eighteen possible species.

But there was another reason. A Fork-tailed Flycatcher is not just your run-of-the-mill unexpected sighting—not even by Cape May standards. It would, in fact, be a North American life bird for four of our party. Yes, including Roger—Number 697.

The Fork-tailed story had started twenty-four hours earlier when a couple had walked into Cape May Bird Observatory and confronted Mary Gustafson and Linda Mills with a story about a bird with a short, forked tail that was either some sort of tern—or "possibly a Fork-tailed Flycatcher." The bird was chasing insects in a plowed field.

Thirty minutes later, Linda was back at CMBO, pouring details into the phone. I was on the other end, in a familiar kitchen in Whippany, New Jersey, offering congratulations and fending off mild attacks of disappointment. A malfunctioning radio had cost me a Fork-tailed Flycatcher in 1978; now, fate, it seemed, had taken another. Linda and Mary were going to call all of the local members of the Cape May birding block (those that stood a chance of getting to Cape May Point before dark) but neither knew how to change the hotline carrying five minutes of information crucial to the thirteen teams competing in the first annual World Series of Birding. Besides, Fork-tailed Flycatchers *never* linger. The bird would be gone for sure on Saturday.

For my part, I didn't give the bird another thought until the members of the Guerrilla Birding Team—Bacinski, Boyle, Peterson, Sibley, and I—met in the lobby of the Old Mill Inn in Bernardsville for one last-minute briefing. One hour later, we were on the old dike road that cuts across the Great Swamp, listening in a cold, penetrating drizzle for a Virginia Rail that never called.

Somewhere under the cover of darkness, twelve other teams of birders were moving like clouds on a moonless night. They were testing their abilities, not because they doubted them, but because our species seems driven to reach for what is just out of reach. What was out of reach was two hundred species of birds in a single day. No birder and no group of birders had ever recorded two hundred or more species, under the sun or moon, in New Jersey—or for that matter in any state except California, Texas, and Alabama.

There are those who snort, stamp their feet, and mutter indignantly about the simplemindedness that makes grown people want to stand in the rain at midnight or crisscross a state, ringing up birds with the abandon of kids at the Easter egg hunt on the White House lawn. "It's not bird-watching," they scream righteously. "It's foolishness." And so it is!

But tomorrow, those same birders who were focusing all of the skills accrued during a lifetime of study onto the location of birds by sight and sound would be standing in the South Cape May meadows, watching the antics of feeding shorebirds or wrapped in a warbler fallout at Higbee Beach—and loving it. The very same ones!

One of the most compelling things about this activity called *birding* is the breadth of its scope. It can accommodate both the hard-core lister and the backyard feeder birder. In fact, it is so generous in its scope that it can, at once, accommodate not only big day birders, but even people who object to them!

Isn't birding wonderful.

Our route carried us to the Black River (for more birds that make noises in the dark) and then to the elevated railroad bed at Waterloo, New Jersey. It was a cold dawn, a gray dawn. The air hung damp and still. Cinders crunched underfoot as we drew abreast of the field flanked by tight formations of hedges. Quickly we formed a line, facing the field with a bloodless dawn at our backs. It was not a hopeful morning for birds.

But this was no ordinary commander marshalling our effort. It was North American Birding Himself who was standing on the roadbed that morning, feet comfortably spaced, head turned slightly askew, his features tense, waiting. And we stood in his shadow, mere knights and rooks in the presence of the Master and as the dawn broadened behind us, we watched his mastery unfold.

"Blue-winged Warbler," he said, jabbing the air with his finger for emphasis and guidance. "Field Sparrow . . . Brown Thrasher . . . catbird . . . Canada Warbler . . . Northern Waterthrush . . . White-throated Sparrow. . . . "

"I missed it," a voice said matter-of-factly.

"There," said Roger.

"Got it," the same voice replied.

"Flicker . . . Chipping Sparrow . . . Yellow-throat . . . Chestnut-sided Warbler. . . ."

"Missed it," another voice said, momentarily stopping the flow. "Where?"

"Behind us," said Roger. "Alternate song," someone else suggested helpfully.

It called again. "Got it."

And these were no ordinary lieutenants flanking the Master, not the Bacinskis and Boyles and Sibleys of this world. One by one, each crucial songster was grabbed by the ears—a distant Worm-eating Warbler, a flyover Purple Finch, a lingering Solitary Vireo (making an off, three-note call)—each bird a small victory, one step closer to two hundred species.

At Princeton's Institute Woods, we were ambushed by a fanatical band of Peterson admirers brandishing a formidable arsenal of unsigned field guides. We barely escaped with our civility intact. At Brigantine National Wildlife Refuge, a CBS camera crew mounted a fifth-column movement—assisted by members of a rival team who intimated to fellow birders that "you-know-who is in that car behind you—but don't tell anyone we told you."

There were great victories along our route—Orange-crowned Warbler . . . Ruddy Duck; and bitter defeats—*No* Summer Tanager! *No* kingfisher! *No* Broad-winged Hawk!!! And, here, now, at the very tip of New Jersey, with our total at 183 species, there was just the slimmest measure of hope that the goal of two hundred species was within our reach. And maybe, just maybe, a Fork-tailed Flycatcher.

We began our retreat through the meadows, according to our fatigue. Quickly we loaded the scopes in the car. Four doors slammed shut with the smartness of a parade-ground salute. The Mercedes moved out of the lot for the short drive up Bayshore Road—our second time up that road today.

The car drew slowly to a stop, midway down the length of a plowed field. The blue whale grinned widely off to our left. Indifferently, I brought my binoculars up and felt the others imitate the gesture. Several kingbirds perched casually on a row of bushes about one hundred yards out—along with a slimmer, longer bird that seemed to have a pale, blue back: Fork-tailed Flycatcher.

"There it is," David said.

"I got it," I said, unable to keep the surprise out of my voice.

The car emptied *immediately*. Five scopes emerged from the trunk amid a frenzy of arms and tripods. At 22x the bird stood out like a Peterson plate: a young bird, lacking the long streamer tail feathers of an adult. Under scrutiny, it made a short sortie into the field, grabbed something, and moved back to take its perch.

"I haven't got it yet," Pete said in tones that barely disguised his anxiety.

"On the ground," I said. "Here, it's in the scope."

David's silence and studied expression left nothing to question. Bill's fine focusing maneuvers at the helm of his Questar overshadowed any doubts from that quarter.

Roger?

His scope stopped moving. His hand touched the focus wheel lightly, and North America's birding patriarch gave his attention to the eyepiece—and whatever lay beyond.

"Yes," he said quietly, intently. "Yes," he said, straightening up, smiling widely. "I've seen the bird, you know, in Mexico. But it is my first for North America."

We knew.

We gave the bird two minutes of study—two minutes more than we had to spare, and left, heading north. There was less than two hours of daylight left. And sixteen species to go.

SVAT

The phone rang once, stopping the six of diamonds and Brian's hand halfway across the table. His eyes strayed instinctively toward the time clock—09:50:44. Before the second ring, he had activated the telephone recorder, noted the time on the Sight Report, and, having no legitimate options, dropped the six of diamonds on the seven of hearts. He lifted the receiver on the second ring.

"SVAT here," he said with all the cheerfulness of a New York City toll booth attendant. "Give your name, your PABLUM Identification Number (if you have one), and your telephone number. Then, give your report."

There was a long pause during which Brian wrote furiously. Nobody else had moved. Sometimes they fielded ten calls an hour at SVAT on a peak weekend—though things had been slow, even for midweek.

"What makes you think Tine-tailed," Brian interrupted brusquely.

He continued to write, using a cryptic series of notations. Cradling the phone with an upraised shoulder, he punched a 12–digit code into the computer. The large overhead screen went nova for a split second and then displayed the upper half of a wholesome-looking, elderly woman wearing turtleshell glasses, her hair tied back in a severe bun. Next to the video image was the all-pertinent data:

NAME: Alberta Rotweiller   AGE: 66   BORN: March 15,
1918
Dismal Seepage, AR

MARITAL STATUS: Widow   RESIDENCE: Platt Flatt, CO

BIRDING DATA:

Classification: Feeder Class 1941–1952
                        Bander Class, jg 1952–present
Affiliations: Polk County Audubon since 1947 (past
                        president)
                    Compiler: Moo County CBC
                    Columnist: Moo County *Crier* "Our
                        Feathered Friends" (Weekly)
Trips: Audubon Camp, Maine, 1948, 1954
            Everglades, 1957
Verified Reports: Blue Jay, feeder bird, December 19,
                        1963–February (sighting confirmed by
                        photos)

NO PREVIOUS SVAT CONTACTS

NO PREVIOUS SVAT DISQUALIFICATIONS

Brian studied the face and the information and made occasional notations on the pad and noncommittal noises into the
mouthpiece of the phone.

"Could I have directions to the site?" he asked.

For the first time, there were some stirrings from the other
bodies in the room. Hans Muller closed the copy of *Birds of the
USSR* and set it next to his bunk. Matthew Roberts glanced
quickly up from the birding simulator video game called
"South Cape May." Down in the training room was Lisa Remington—the fourth and final member of SVAT, Species Verification Attack Team, the crack investigative attack force of
PABLUM, Pure American Bird Listers Uber-Membership.

Ten years ago, there was no SVAT. The scramble for 700 species of birds in North America could only be accomplished
through lavish amounts of hard birding—an unproductive and
time-consuming business. Sighting information networks
were uncoordinated. Hotlines were updated after the fact, and
unless a continent-trotting lister wanted to call every hotline
in North America, he or she might never hear about the Spade-

billed Sandpiper in Oregon or the Mauve-colored Thrush in Texas. What's more, in order to get to these avian gems, a caller often had to wade through a bin of verbal chaff—CBC results, the dates of the next bird seed sale, or reports on common North American birds that had simply wandered to someplace else within the continent. The situation had grown so desperate that Attu-Class birders were reduced to having to forgo birding on weekends. Leaving the phone ran the risk of missing reports of key sightings.

Each one a specialist; each one an expert.

On top of all of this adversity was the ever-present threat of misidentification. Many a needy lister had traveled thousands of miles only to discover that an aspired-to avian waif was merely an oiled yellowlegs or worse—to *not* make the discovery and rubber-stamp a boo-boo. It was the Siberian Tic debacle in Ontario that proved the catalyst. Hundreds made the trek to see the celebrated feeder bird, only to discover weeks later that the bird was, in reality, a melanistic Charcoal-capped Chickadee.

Birding's credibility was on the ropes. The need for a continental communication network and an infallible species verification system was paramount. SVAT, a crack team of identification experts that could be on site in hours was the child of this desperation.

Funding for the project came from matching grants by three airlines, two car rental agencies, and half a dozen motel chains. Solicitation and screening of prospective SVAT candidates were conducted by a stellar PABLUM search committee. Over 1,100 applications were submitted; better than three hundred were interviewed. Four were chosen—the cream of the cream, each one a specialist, each one an expert.

Hans (Wolfgang) Muller, Team Leader (formerly Hans Müller)
Age: 67   Born: July 19, 1917, Dresden, Germany
Marital Status: Disputed
Education: Records lost
Birding Data: CLASSIFICATION: Eilat Class
Birding Experience: Germany 1923–1939
                      Poland 1939–1944
                      Switzerland 1945–1946
                      UNKNOWN 1946–1948
                      Argentina 1949–1951
                      Bolivia 1952–1953
                      Brazil 1953–1977
                      United States of America 1977–present
Specialty: European and Neotropical Species;
             Intercontinental Flight; Witness Interrogation

Matthew (Freeze-frame) Roberts
Age: 19   Born: March 1, 1965, Los Angeles, California
Marital Status: Single
Education: Maharishi Country Day School 1967–1969
            K-10, Los Angeles Public School System
            1970–1981
            (2 years each in 2nd and 5th grade)
Work Experience: Consultant to Apple, Inc.; Nikon; Atari;
            U.S. Department of Defense 1980–
            Present
Birding Data: CLASSIFICATION: Attu Class
Birding Experience: California 1973–1983
            One trip to Disney World 1975
Specialty: Western North American Species; Photography;
            Communications Systems; Electronics; Computer
            Systems

Brian
Age: Classified   Born: (Date Classified); Location (Classified)
Education: K-12 Public School System (Location Classified)
            University of California (Berkeley) 1969–1971
Military Experience: Enlisted Army Airborne 1959
            Ranger Training 1960
            Special Forces 1960–1966 (3 tours of
            Viet Nam)
            Honors: Distinguished Service Medal;
                Bronze Star (2) Silver Star (2);
                Congressionl Medal of Honor;
                Purple Heart (5)
            Dishonorable Discharge 1966
            1967–1969 Classified (at request of
            CIA)
Birding Data: CLASSIFICATION: Eilat Class
Birding Experience: Southeast Asia 1960–1966
            Israel, Egypt, Syria 1967–1968
            Dominican Republic 1968
            California 1969–1971

> Canada 1972–1973
> Chile 1973–1975
> Iran 1976–1979
> Nicaragua 1980–1982
> Grenada 1983

Specialty: Asian, Middle Eastern, South American species with a specialty in nocturnals; Demolition (all forms)

Lisa Remington
Age: 27 Born: August 14, 1957, Mystic, CT
Marital Status: Single
Education: Monticello School for Young Ladies 1963–1973
Switzerland 1973–1974
Bryn Mawr 1974–1978
Military Experience: U.S. Air Force 1978–1980
Work Experience: NASA Space Shuttle Program Trainer 1980
Geothermal Life Research Project (diver) 1981–1982
Consultant/Trainer British Amphibious Assault Forces 1983
Nolls Trainer (Tec. climbing, diving, spelunking) 1983
Formula Ford Circuit Driver 1983–1984
Birding Data: CLASSIFICATION: Attu Class
Birding Experience: "Well, everywhere."
Specialty: Navigation (yachting); Small Aircraft; Driving; Skydiving; Downhill Skiing; Flight Identification

Since the inception of the team in 1983, they had fielded 3,474 calls; conducted 306 on-site investigations, and confirmed the identification of 66 Code-5 rarities.

They have never failed to reach a prime prospect anywhere in North America in more than twelve hours. They have never failed to confirm or negate a tentative identification. They have never misidentified a target sighting (based on the analysis of photographs taken on site by experts). And, most importantly, they have never failed to fulfill their prime objective. They have never failed to alert the card-carrying members of PABLUM in time. It was SVAT, purely SVAT, that had put North American bird listers on the edge of a new frontier—the 800 Club.

"Are you going to be at this location all day and can we reach you if there is need for further contact?" Brian inquired.

There was a short pause during which he switched off the screen and pushed the ALERT button, linking SVAT Central to the training room.

"Thank you for your report," he said. "You're a credit to the birding community." There was a pause . . . and then Brian said, "Yes, ma'am . . . that would be very nice, ma'am . . . " And then, with a trace of impatience, "No, ma'am, it's more important that you stay on site . . . yes, milk will be fine. Yes. Thank you."

He hung up the phone.

"Vas ist los?" Hans inquired gruffly.

Brian spun around to face the balding, overweight, son of a cuckoo-clock maker who hadn't slept a full night in nearly forty years (and looked every bit of it).

"A Mrs. Alberta Rotweiller believes she has an adult Tine-tailed Gnatsnatcher. The bird was first seen at 0630 this morning near Rio Grande. Her initial identification was Serpent-tongued Gnatsnatcher but she was confused by the dark cap. After consulting the New Eastern Peterson's guide and making several trips back to the site, she called a local Audubon Center, who gave her our number."

Herr Muller snorted derisively. "It ist der Oestern Kingbird most likely. Krazy der dicky-birders vil drive us mit der shtupid reports."

Brian looked evenly at the pasty features of his commander's face (horribly deformed by too much of the good life). "I think the report has merit," he replied. "One, the woman originally comes from an area where Serpent-tongued is common. Two, the report-site has a history of Tine-tailed sightings. Three, the description was convincing; the bird is hard to misidentify. Four, though relatively inexperienced, the woman has no record of irresponsible sightings or reports."

While Brian enumerated his points, Hans paced monotonously back and forth in a histrionic display of deep concentration. The truth was, Hans had no gift for sifting reports and had learned to rely on Brian's cool and even reasoning powers.

At that moment, the door to the Command Center burst open. A strikingly pretty, petite young woman wearing a jump suit that was at least 80% Velcro pounced into the room. Landing on the balls of her feet in a half crouch, she kicked off with her left foot and brought it up over her head. In the same fluid motion, she brought her custom Leitz 10 x 40s to bear on Brian, then Hans, and then (twisting herself back the other way, against the flow of her body) on Matthew—a split second before her foot touched the light switch, plunging the room into darkness.

The sound of a body tumbling easily into a bunk was drowned out by Matthew's cries of rage and Hans's Teutonic invectives. Brian coolly touched the emergency light switch; it revealed Lisa reclining easily on her bunk, calmly working her binoculars over with an airbrush and removing nonexistent dust particles. Openly displayed just below her shoulder was the SVAT arm patch, the logo that had, in just six months, become part of the birding vernacular: IN GOD WE TRUST. ALL OTHERS BETTER PRODUCE THE SPECIMEN.

The light also confirmed Matthew's greatest fear. During the blackout, he had lost the video game. In "South Cape May," the player attempts to snap-identify fast-moving avian forms without being run over in the parking lot, electrocuted on the cattle fence, or maimed by fellow birders, and without stepping in a cow pie. Finally, identifications have to be made before the shorts-and-sneaker-clad phantom birder pops out of the bushes and beats you to the call. Matthew's video effigy was standing squarely in a very nasty video-enhanced cow pie.

GAME OVER.

Doing a very convincing impersonation of an enraged praying mantis, Matthew stalked to the edge of Lisa's bunk and spewed a mixture of sounds, words, and spittle.

"Why, you pre-pre-preppy li-little twi-twi-twi-twit! You made me lose THE GAME!!!"

Lisa looked up, smiled sweetly, and said, "Why don't you go skateboarding on a freeway."

Matthew made a strangling sound and screamed: "TART!!!"

"Creep," Lisa offered.

"BITCH!!!"

"Jerk," she observed brightly.

"ICE QUEEN!"

The smile stayed on Lisa's face but the sweetness had gone elsewhere. Those emerald eyes that made everyone look twice drew into two narrow slits. Her stomach tightened and both hands closed slowly into fists.

"She's going to kill him," Brian thought—and she probably would have, had not Hans's authoritarian impulses carried him between the polarized pair.

"Shtop mit der name callings, here," he demanded. "It ist like der two babies ve have. Ya, baby one und baby two. Ve have der work to do und dat is vat ve do here; not der baby playing."

Some of the sweetness returned to Lisa's face. "Oh, Hans," she said, "you are so right, of course. I'm sorry to be such an added burden to you on top of all of your other responsibilities. I don't know what comes over me. I just get *so* carried away right before action," she concluded, serenely, turning herself to look fully into her Commander's face. "I'm sorry about your game, Matthew," she consoled with the sincerity of a banker foreclosing a mortgage—and she smiled, showing just a tad too much canine to be really convincing.

Hans nodded approvingly and turned away. "Ya, *dat* ist der maturity dat ist der hallmark of der gut teamwork." He didn't see Lisa and Matthew's exchange of obscene gestures.

"What's the scoop?" Lisa inquired, her voice now clipped and businesslike.

Quickly, Brian gave her a rundown while Matthew transferred all pertinent details onto a cassette. If the sighting was confirmed, the tape would convey the information to the PABLUM rank and file. Absently, he punched 442.1 into the computer section marked: SPECIES. A full readout on Tine-tailed appeared.

TINE-TAILED GNATSNATCHER, (*Muscivora obitinass*) CODE 5 RARITY. Length: 14 in (35 cm). Description: Medium-sized flycatcher; superficially resembles Eastern Kingbird with a long, forked streamer tail (adults only). Head and sides of face: black; wings and tail: black. Back: pale gray. Underparts: white.
Several subspecies recognized. DISTRIBUTION AND RANGE: From Veracruz (Mexico) through Central and South America to Patagonia. The nominate race migrates extensively northward after breeding to northern South America. Accidental to Bermuda. PABLUM ZONE RECORDS: 40 + records between 1820–1983. Sightings/State: NJ 8; TX 6; ME 5; MA 5; NY 3; FL and NS 2; MS, WI, GA, ONT, MD, and NB 1. Periods of Occurrence: July–November. Spring: March (1), May (2).

Turning to Matthew, Hans said, "Put der Ubermembers on der first alert; condition YELLOW. Der Tine-tailed ist ein slippery devil, und if der verification ist gut, der members vil not much time have."

Matthew punched a complicated sequence into the computer and in the flick of a switch, five thousand beepers went off in five thousand pockets, putting five thousand PABLUM members on notice that an abrupt change in their schedules was in the offing. All members who already *had* Tine-tailed on their North American list were, of course, excluded.

Spinning to face Lisa, Hans said: "Der Falcon 10 ist fueled und ready." It was a statement, not a question.

Lisa stood up, smiled sadly, and said, apologetically, "Well, yes and no . . ."

"Vat do you mean 'yes und no?'" Hans interrupted. "Der plane ist ready or ist not ready. Ya or nein?"

"Nein," she sighed. "I mean, no," she said, lifting her shoulders in a gesture of helplessness. "The jet is in the hanger being outfitted with a new guidance system. It's been quiet lately and global weather maps didn't show patterns that should have produced anything significant," she added defensively (trying to ignore the wide smile on Matthew's face—and failing).

"It had to be done *sometime*," she concluded, her voice climbing about two octaves.

Hans said a few choice things in German and then, "Den ve will der jet copter have to use."

Lisa winced and said in a barely audible voice, "Uh, the copter hasn't been cleared since the rotor strike, Hans."

"Since the Siberian Crane rotor strike," Matthew added (for the sake of accuracy).

Lisa sighed. Nobody said anything for an uncomfortable few moments and the floor seemed to have become an object of fascination.

When they looked up, Hans was vibrating like a miniature Vesuvius and making a noise like the sound that comes out of a Doberman's throat when its mouth is full of forearm. He made a superhuman effort to gain control. Failing this, he simply exploded and emitted a series of Germanic sounds, some of which were words.

"UND VAT IST VE TO DO TO GET DER? VE CAN VALK I SUPPOSE, YA? VE CAN MAYBE POST OURSELVES UND GET DER EXPRESS MAIL? DER DUMKOPH DAT FIXES DER PLANE VEN DER COPTER IST KAPUT SHOOTING IST TOO GUT FOR. DER RUSSIAN FRONT I VIL SEND YOU—YA, BAREFOOT!"

It was at this critical junction, when life and death were on the line, that Brian interrupted.

"Hans?"

"YA!"

"Hans, if you'd like, we can use my car and drive to the site," he said calmly.

Hans looked at him like the nose had fallen off his face. "To Texas you vil drive from Cape May und by nightfall get there? Der loony-bin you vil drive to, not der Texas."

Brian's expression didn't change. He continued, coolly as ever, "Who said anything about *Texas*? The bird is in Rio Grande, *New Jersey*. Mrs. Rotweiller is visiting her daughter in Rio Grande and saw the bird there. We can get there in fifteen minutes—as long as you don't mind stopping for gas. I'm nearly on 'E.' "

The unmarked beige sedan pulled up beneath the stately Spanish oaks halfway between the white frame house and the garage. Mrs. Rotweiller appeared immediately, wiping her hands on an apron bedecked with the standard assortment of cardinals, chickadees, grosbeaks, and male goldfinches in breeding plumage. She took the porch steps one at a time, always leading with her right. A problem with her left hip, Brian surmised. She was a tad heavier than her picture showed (most of the added ballast was packed in the stern). She wore the standard-issue gingham skirt, hand-knit wool sweater, L.L. Bean walking shoes, and a pair of Bausch and Lomb 7x35 Zephyrs showing lots of metal. She was smiling widely and though still over seventy feet away, already talking.

"Oh, you got here so quickly," she said a little breathlessly. "Why, the brownies haven't gone in yet and I haven't started the coffee because I wanted it to be fresh and I'm Alberta Rotweiller and this is *such* a thrill for me and . . . and . . . an *honor*," she added (mostly addressing Hans, now).

She plumped her bun lightly and stopped directly in front of the beaming team leader (about a foot closer than purely social motives would account for). Herr Muller brought his heels together smartly, bowed stiffly, and, taking the hand dangling suggestively about two inches from his nose, brought it lightly to his lips. "Der pleasure, it ist all mine, of course, ven der beautiful lady introduced ist," he said grandly.

Matthew rolled his eyes in a sweeping arch that covered about 260 degrees and slouched with just a little more defiance. Brian was studying the large plowed field north of the house.

Lisa offered her most disarming smile and said, "Oh, what a

beautiful sweater, and such a complicated pattern. Did you choose the color or was the wool on sale?"

Alberta may have been a simple soul but she wasn't stupid, and she'd fielded debutantes before. Matching Lisa's smile in sweetness and venom, she said, "No dearie, God picks the color; we just grow the sheep."

"He has such good taste," Lisa said admiringly—wrinkling her nose only slightly.

"Yes, doesn't He, though," Alberta said in tones that would have put even a mild diabetic into a coma. She returned her attention to Hans, who'd missed the whole parry and thrust.

"Oh, Herr Muller," she continued, breathlessly, "I saw you speak at the WBBA Convention in Steamboat Springs several years ago on the identification of those little flycatchers with wing bars—based on the kinds of . . . of . . . bugs, or something, that they carry around under their feathers. It was all very fascinating," she added in a fashion that made it obvious that she didn't have the faintest idea of what he'd been talking about. It didn't really matter. Neither did Hans.

"Ya, ya, der Rhinobassid Fly," he pronounced wisely. "A tremendous possibility der, ya, to tell der dicky flycatchers from der other dicky flycatchers by der flies I.D. Vy der ist every reason to believe dat . . ."

Recognizing the danger, Brian interrupted. "The bird you reported is in that field over there?" he inquired of Alberta.

"Why, yes," she acknowledged. "He was feeding around that little island of trees in the middle. I haven't seem him in over an hour though," she added. "Oh, I hope he hasn't disappeared. Or been frightened away."

"I recall from NORAD photos," Brian continued, "that there is a small clearing in the middle of the grove—a field, perhaps?"

"Uh, why, yes," Mrs. Rotweiller replied (a little startled, it seemed). "My, uh, nephew and some of his friends had a, well, small garden in there about ten years ago—but all that was cleared up years ago."

Brian turned to Hans. "Sir, I suspect that the bird is using that patch. It's cool and a little on the windy side and there isn't much insect action on the side that we can see. The sun is high enough now to warm the clearing. It would be a perfect place for the bird, given the conditions and its habits."

"Ya, exactly vat I was thinking," Hans pronounced.

"The only thing that puzzles me," Brian continued, looking back at Alberta, "is why the bird went in deep. The south side of that island is out of the wind and I assume," he said, addressing Mrs. Rotweiller, "that *that* is where the bird was seen originally."

Mrs. Rotweiller, who seemed suddenly to have noticed that the daffodils needed trimming, merely nodded. She seemed oddly uncommunicative.

Brian waited a moment or two before continuing. "Uh, do I recall that you run a small songbird-banding operation on your ranch?" he probed gently.

Another nod.

Brian cleared his throat, uncomfortably, but it was Matthew who laid it all out on the floor.

"YOU DIDN'T BAND THE BIRD, DID YOU?!" he screeched.

Alberta's head dropped like she just took the executioner's ax. Her chin trembled and both tear ducts burst at the seams.

"N-n-n-no," she said, brokenly. "Ah, ah, I strung . . . a net . . . where the bird . . . wa, wa, was f-feeding." She sniffed grandly, accepted the handkerchief offered by Hans, and blew a hearty toot. Composing herself, she continued. "The bird went into the second trammel but the mesh was too small, I guess. It flew right down the bag and got out the end. It went into the island . . . and I haven't seen it since," she concluded, her words trailing off into a very embarrassed silence.

"Der, der," Hans consoled. "Der vast no harm done, I think. It vast der Devil made you do it, ya? So long as you did not TOUCH der bird, nicht vas?"

"No," she said. "It got away. I just thought that if I could catch it, then it could be verified with photos."

Hans's manner changed abruptly. "NEIN, NEIN, NEIN, NEIN, NEIN. *DAT* ist der bolshevik talk. *DAT* is der near *shot-*

gun think. It ist for der SVAT to make der identification und to alert der birders. *DAT* ist der vay dat birding should be conducted. DAT is vy SVAT ist."

Alberta sniffed, nodded contritely, and mustered a wan smile. Satisfied that the lesson had been learned, Hans grasped her firmly by the fleshy part of the arm and escorted her toward the porch.

"Gut, gut. Ve just forget der whole thing, ya? Der finger dat ist burnt once ist two times gets der varning, ya? Ready maybe ist der brownies? Der verk ve must now do und den maybe der delights, ya?" he added rather ambiguously.

Alberta cantered toward the house, grateful for the opportunity to lose herself in something important. She turned and called back to the retreating German. "Oh, Hans. Do you like your brownies with or without nuts?"

Hans answered unhesitantly. "Always mit der nuts," he said and smiled.

Alberta blew Hans a kiss and waved vigorously. Hans returned the gesture with a flourish that betrayed both his aristocratic lines and political roots, and he marched rather stiffly toward his attack force.

Matthew and Lisa winced and exchanged knowing glances. They might have been worlds apart on most matters, but they were of one mind when it came to Hans.

Hermann Goering's self-styled twin reached his team and immediately began rattling off orders in garbled German and English—most of them contradictory. It didn't make much difference. The setup was pretty cut and dried—in fact, it was almost identical to the Speckled Crake affair two weeks earlier. They had only *just* received the briefs from the landowner's lawyers on that one.

"Ve vil set up der command post here," Hans said, planting the heel of one hobnailed boot for guidance and drama. "Der fire line down at der fence, ya," he said, indicating a spot some 100 yards closer to the spot where the bird was last seen.

Matthew interrupted. "Hans, these things gotta go," he said, pointing to the two stately trees guarding the edge of the field. "If the bird bolts left or right, they'll be right in the fire zone."

91

Hans surveyed the situation and nodded in agreement. "Ya, der big trees, der. . . . Wie heissen sie?" he said, turning to Brian.

"Holly, American holly," he replied. "*Illus opaca.* Beautiful, aren't they," he added (without much hope).

"Ya," Hans agreed, "der holly; Lisa vil take down—to fall away from der bird island, ya?" he said, addressing her directly.

"Doch," she said.

"Der containment charges?" Hans inquired, turning back to Brian. "Der ist no problem?"

"No problem," Brian confirmed.

"Den all ist vell. Everybody now to synchronize der watches. Ist 11:23:30. Ve go at noon. I stay here und keep der watch und answer der questions. OK—everybody rause. Arbeit macht frei," he added enthusiastically but unnecessarily.

Brian picked up his pack and started for the field, keeping well against the woods. Lisa and Matthew headed back to the car. A small throng of birders (no doubt alerted by the local Audubon chapter that had first fielded Alberta's call) were already gathering. The two SVAT team members smiled graciously, politely waved away the several field guides extended their way for autographs, and dodged a flurry of questions.

"Is it Tine-tailed?"

"Have you seen it?"

"Where is it supposed to be?"

"Where are you going to set up the Observer Zone?"

Lisa extracted a bull chainsaw from the trunk, noted some wear on the patented "whisper-gauge" muffler system, and substituted a spare. Matthew extracted two formidable-looking custom camera cases, several tripods, and three large metal film canisters. Looking over the group, he asked for "one" volunteer. Half of those present stepped forward. Matthew selected one carrying a Novaflex system and generously allowed him to carry the two heavier parcels. Lisa was already sending pure white wood chips flying at the base of the first tree.

Humming a catchy and fast climbing top-40s tune that nobody would remember in three weeks, Matthew and his photogaboon reached the firing line and began setting up the hypersophisticated photo-capture system—a system so new and so state-of-the-art that the CIA and KGB were still stealing the prototype designs from each other's agents. Matthew had scrapped *that* system nearly a week ago.

There would be three separate camera units, each operating independently of the other to reduce any chance of a blanket malfunction. Two 600mm/ wide-angle units, one loaded with black-and-white film and the other with color slides, would scour the area in continuous 180-degree sweeps while shooting ninety frames a second. The camera bodies and magnum film packs were constructed from a special heat-resistant alloy to prevent a meltdown. The third camera was equipped with a top secret, laser sensor/tracker designed to locate, focus on, and follow any bird whose flight rhythms and movements were preprogrammed into the unit. It would alternately shoot frames of Tri-X 400, Kodachrome 64, Infrared, and Polaroid self-developing film.

Every fifth shot was a tracer.

Matthew surveyed the setup with a critical eye and noted, happily, that Lisa was well into the second tree and that she was even troubling to top off some of the more offensive limbs.

"I'm a volunteer at the local Audubon Center," Matthew's assistant said, just to break the ice a little.

"Terrific," Matthew observed without too much enthusiasm.

"So how long have you been watching birds?" the fellow asked conversationally.

"I don't watch birds," Matthew replied simply. "I just identify them. Let's go."

Brian, too, was well along in his appointed task. The charges two hundred feet to the left and behind the island of trees were already planted—a special formula designed for big bang and big flash but low shrapnel.

You can't count a dead bird.

Crouching low, Matthew sprinted to Brian's side to lend assistance. Brian was just starting to lay the final charge.

While Matthew watched, he reached his hand into a lock-top

plastic bag and removed a fistful of a yellow, putty-like substance. Hefting it for weight, he pinched off what he apparently regarded to be excess, molded the balance of the explosive into a compact ball, and placed it squarely onto a paper plate nestled in a shallow depression thirty feet from the other charge already in place. Taking an innocuous cylinder from a pocket sewed into the inside of his pack, he inserted the end of a thin, black wire, crimped the top, and pressed the cylinder firmly into the center of the explosive. Every movement was precise and sure.

Matthew clucked his tongue approvingly. "Sure do love to watch a professional work," he said admiringly. "Where'd you learn to string explosives like that?" he asked. "Nam?"

"No, Berkeley," Brian replied wryly (but truthfully). "We had a bigger budget in Nam."

"Why don't you bury the charges a little deeper?" Matthew queried. "That's the way they do it on television."

"Because," Brian explained (as best he could with a wire between his teeth), "we just want to make a bang, not blow up a train. Throw a lot of dirt and gravel around and someone is liable to get hurt."

"Or some*thing*," Matthew corrected.

"Or something," Brian agreed.

"Seen it?" Matthew asked.

"No. You?"

"Uh, uh," Matthew replied. He paused uncertainly, then asked, "Think it's really in there?"

Brian paused for a thoughtful few seconds, glanced at his watch, and hurriedly started to pack.

"I don't know," he said honestly.

"Do you think it was Tine-tailed?" Matthew asked, not wanting to let it go.

"I don't know that either," Brian quipped, "but we'll know in seven minutes and forty seconds. Here, take these two lines, this one in your left hand, this one in your right—and don't mix them up. Let's go."

They beat Lisa back to the command post by two steps.

Hans was waiting impatiently (even though they were fully a

minute ahead of schedule). The sandbags and medium-range mortar (along with an ample supply of rounds) were already in place. David started to hook the wires to the fire control box.

"All ist ready?" Hans inquired.

Nods all around.

"Der bird is not by anyone seen?"

Anti-nods all around.

"Mat-thew," he said. "To der house go und get der paper signed, und be quick."

Matthew's knock was answered immediately by a very noisy collie and moments later by Mrs. Rotweiller.

"Oh," she said, with a trace of disapointment and a glance over Matthew's shoulder. "Does your commander need anything?"

"Yes, ma'am," Matthew replied, trying his best not to sound like a used car salesman. "Could you please sign this? It's merely a formality."

She took the somewhat official-looking document and squinted hard at it. "I left my reading glasses in the kitchen," she confided. "What is it?" she asked, trying at the same time to make out the bold-faced, capital letters which read: COVENANT NOT TO SUE OR MAKE CLAIM, INDEMNIFICATION CONTRACT AND RELEASE FROM LIABILITY.

"Oh, just something that says that you called us, and that we came to identify the bird just like you wanted," Matthew said, reaching down to pet the collie while he admired a family portrait and whistled a few bars of "Amazing Grace."

"Hmmmm," she said, obviously worried. "I really don't know anything about these things. My late husband used to handle all of the paperwork." She looked sharply at Matthew. "I won't be put on any mailing lists, will I?" she asked, pointedly.

"Oh, *no* ma'am," Matthew assured her in tones that suggested that he was horrified that she would consider such a thing.

"Well . . . all right, then," Alberta said, obviously reassured. "If Hans thinks it's important, it must be important."

"You don't know the half of it," Matthew muttered under his breath.

"What did you say?"

"I said, don't forget to sign the back of it," he said, loudly.

"No, of course," she replied, turning the document over and penning her signature. Matthew took the paper like Judas pocketing his silver and beat it for the porch. Mrs. Rotweiller's voice followed him out the door. ·

"Oh, tell Hans and the others that I'm making fudge icing to put on the brownies. He does like icing, I hope?"

"Loves it," Matthew replied over his shoulder. "Puts it on everything. Thanks." He reached the command post with forty seconds to spare.

"All ist in order?" Hans inquired hopefully.

"Piece of cake," Matthew quipped, turning the release over to his boss, who grunted his approval and pocketed the paper.

"Any sign of the bird?"

"Nein. OK—der battle stations. Dis ist der final countdown." Hans reared up like a bear in a blueberry patch. He placed a sterling silver whistle into his mouth and blew three loud blasts. The dozen onlookers crouched behind their cars. Mrs. Rotweiller waved enthusiastically from the kitchen window.

Matthew brought his 10 x 40s up to bear on the trees some 150 yards away and cradled the remote triggering release in his right hand. Lisa crouched next to the mortar, eyes bright, mouth parted slightly, the tip of her tongue nervously tracing the edge of her teeth. The rocket-shaped projectile in her hand was poised over the muzzle.

Brian was lying quietly with his right hand on the mortar's trajectory control, his chin resting comfortably on the back of the other. The sun that was hot on the back of his neck had already burned away the dew that had lain heavy in the shadows on their arrival. On the far side of the field, two male yellow warblers were chasing each other around, two yellow sparks set against the dogwoods that were just coming into bloom. As he watched, an Osprey came in with prey and took a perch in a dead cedar on the island. "A weakie," Brian mused. "Weakies should be in the bay by now." As he watched, the bird pulled one long, silver strip free, and then another.

"Range, oh, four, double oh," Hans proclaimed. Brian punched each number into the fire control as it was spoken.

"Everything now ist right?" Hans queried, but did not look to see the heads nod around him. His eyes were on the thin, red spoke of his watch that was moving very quickly now to meet the two other darker spokes already joined at twelve.

The Osprey pulled another strip of fish free and bolted it down.

"Fire."

The mortar jumped spasmodically, and at the far end of the field, two dogwoods shed their leaves and most of their limbs simultaneously. They felt the explosion beneath them before they heard the sound that rocked every building on the farm.

KA-WHOOM.

One of the warblers drew a yellow line across the field. The Osprey executed a backward somersault off its perch; the weakfish did a two and one-half gainer going the other way (but neither would have scored very high).

Mrs. Rotweiller, making full use of her ballast distribution, leaned out the kitchen window and shouted, "Mercy sakes alive!" (along with something that would have given the Platt Flatt Lutheran minister a coronary). "Hans!" she screamed, "Hans, what are you doing?"

"Ya, ya," he said. "Everything ist fine. Vat is dat I smell? Ist der brownies burning I hope not?"

Alberta reacted like a knee assaulted by a hammer, and she disappeared.

"Any sign of der bird?" Hans demanded.

"Negative," Matthew replied.

"Add five degrees right, und drop 100 yards," Hans commanded.

"Fire."

The mortar bucked again and a dark tower of topsoil appeared halfway between the distant tree line and the center island.

KA-WHOOM.

An unusually quiet collie wearing half a screen door went across the driveway at a dead run as about twenty bushels of seedling corn started its descent back to earth.

"Hans!"

Mrs. Rotweiller, now wearing an old Civil Defense helmet that some trunk had surrendered, was standing on the porch.

"Hans, have you lost your mind? You aren't blowing up the farm, are you?"

"Nein, nein, nein, nein, nein," he shouted back, waving reassuringly. "Ve vil be through here in just der jiffy. Der koffee it smells wonderful. Ist done? I like mit cream und three sugars."

"But the person I talked to on the phone said that milk would be fine. I didn't go out for cream."

"Ya, der milk ist fine. But hurry, ve ist finished nearly. Vas ist los?" he said, turning his attention back to the battle.

"Nothing," Matthew said.

"Drop der hundred yards, den."

"That will put it very close," Brian cautioned.

"Here, I give der commands," Hans said sharply, in no mood for insubordination. "Ready?"

"Ya," Brian said, more a sigh than a word.

"Fire, den."

The round appeared to drop just on the back side of the grove; it sent up a shower of dirt and leaves—and a single, black-and-white, streamer-tailed bird.

"Der Tine-tailed! Der Tine-tailed!" Hans shouted victoriously and danced an excited little jig. "Mat-thew. Mat-thew. Quick. Der cameras."

The bird perched momentarily on top of a newly denuded twig and then started to fly to the left. Brian touched the button marked L-1, which set off the containment charge directly in front of the bird.

Blam.

The bird spun 180 degrees, almost took a perch again, then thought better of it and kept heading east. Brian detonated R-1.

Blam.

It is to the credit of Tine-tailed Gnatsnatchers that they can modify their plans quickly. The bird spun around and returned to the last place on this earth where it had been unmolested—the twig over the island fortress.

"Ya," Hans exclaimed grandly, his spirits carried aloft by success. "Ya, *dat* ist der way der professionals do it. Dat ist der vay dat birding should be conducted."

Lisa and Brian were already breaking down the command post. Matthew was enroute to salvage his still-smoking cameras.

In ten minutes, they were packed. Just before leaving, Matthew planted a battery-operated homing device at the CP site and activated it. Five thousand beepers went off in five thousand pockets of five thousand PABLUM members and in seconds, all lines into SVAT headquarters were jammed with members desperate to learn about the new twitch in the offing, even though the system could handle 1,500 calls a minute.

"I sure hope Auntie Em over there likes company," Lisa mused sardonically as she turned the glossy snapshot and pen over to Matthew.

"I hope she made plenty of brownies," Matthew replied, affixing his John Hancock and pocketing the pen (Lisa's pen). He walked over to the recently vacated CP and placed the autographed 8 x 10 glossy print of a perched, adult, Tine-tailed Gnatsnatcher—a prize for the first out-of-state PABLUM member to reach the site.

Collect three and win a SVAT T-shirt.

Mrs. Rotweiller came out bearing a Corningware percolator and a very full tray of brownies. She stopped when she saw the vacant command post and only then noticed that the beige sedan was no longer there. In fact, the only person in sight was the gentleman who volunteered at the Audubon Center. He was down near the fence watching the bird.

She didn't move for a moment, a little puzzled and a little unhappy and a little uncertain about what to do. She decided to go down and offer the fellow (whose name she couldn't remember) a brownie. She hoped he liked walnuts. And icing.

A Peregrine Going South
for the First Time Again

The bird opened her eyes, and this was the only sign that she had wakened (not, of course, that sleepfulness is ever far from wakefulness in a Peregrine). From her perch on the narrow ledge, she absorbed the world through the dark portals of her eyes in typical Peregrine fashion, taking in both the familiar and unfamiliar, sifting the consequential from the inconsequential.

Before and below her was water, a bay. Beyond, stretching south and slightly east as far as her vision could carry, was the coastline. This was the direction in which she was headed. To the east, where the sea was beginning to glow in anticipation of the sun, lay a town.

The bird had seen more and more of these. She avoided them if it was convenient to do so. They were cramped and cluttered and lacking in prey. There were also numbers of people associated with them—a factor to be considered. Seeing the town brought to mind her first encounter with one of these people—on *the* ledge overlooking *the* river. On her leg, still drawn tight against her breast feathers, was a token of this first meeting.

The name of *the* river was the Coleville and its course bisects the North Slope of Alaska until it spills its waters into the Arctic Ocean. The bird, of course, did not know the name. And the man was Bob Dittrick, a biologist contracted by the U.S. Fish and Wildlife Service to survey the region for nesting Peregrines—but the bird did not know this, either. A name has no bearing on its object, no cause and no effect, and therefore no meaning for a Peregrine. A Peregrine is *all* cause and effect.

100

The bird knew that it was *the* river, and in the razor-apt clarity of her kind could recall every outcropping of shale, every coal seam, boulder, pipit nest, tundra pool, and gravel bar that was there and had bearing on her and her existence (because to a Peregrine, these are one and the same).

The memory of a Peregrine Falcon is not dim, as some have said. For a large part of the world that we perceive (and a measure that we do not), it is precise and direct as point-to-point flight. Things that are important fall neatly into the data-ready channels that genetics and evolution have provided. A Peregrine's memory is only dim where evolution has laid down no paths—for the naming of rivers, for instance.

Another aspect of Peregrine memory that a human would find strange is the time sense—or lack of it. For the bird, there was nothing to distinguish the cotton grass that sheltered her nest ledge and the three brothers who shared it with her from the man she could see walking on the beach with his dog or the sun that was only now cresting the horizon south of the town. Cotton grass on ledges and men who walk dogs on beaches are realities that are merely separated by distance and time—and what concerns are these to the like of a Peregrine Falcon. Facts are facts whenever and wherever they occur.

The sun washed the narrow ledge and the bird; it burnished her darkly streaked underparts with copper. Her face was highlighted by the dark sideburn-slash of her kind, and her head was the color of dwarf willow in autumn. She was a tundra Peregrine, and with or without the sun she was beautiful. This was her first trip south, though in the pathways of her mind she had done this thing countless hundreds of times before.

She had come in off the ocean in the last light of evening and found roost on this odd cliff as much by the lights cast from the town as by the rays of the dying sun. The cliff offered a measure of familiarity in a place where everything was marred by the unknown. It was the most comfortable perch that she had taken since leaving the Arctic—a long, wandering journey that had seen roosts, among other places, on the radio antenna of a Soviet research vessel and a grain elevator near Churchill, Manitoba. In her travels she had encountered many thousands

101

Sitting peregrine

of other birds stirred to restlessness of movement and among them she had encountered many other Peregrines, adults and immatures like herself.

The bird could not have known, of course, that a decade ago, this would not have been the case—or why. The channels of her mind had no place to absorb abstracts like pesticide poisoning, reproductive failure, or species decline. The crash of her kind, and its recovery, occurred in a flash of evolutionary time—too fast for genetic channels to be laid down by survivors. She could not have known that by 1975, the Arctic population had been reduced by more than half and that on *the* river only thirteen pairs of Peregrines attempted to breed. In 1982, there were twenty-six pairs, and these produced forty-eight young. She was one of these.

The biologist Dittrick understood both the decline and the recovery because it is the nature of biologists to know these things, and because for three years he had surveyed *the* river. Before that, he had manned banding stations along the Atlantic Coast. He knew that other biologists working on the Gulf Coast in Texas had taken blood samples from Peregrines returning from tropical wintering grounds. These samples showed that between 1979 and 1980 alone, there were significant reductions in the level of DDE in the birds examined and that less than ten percent of returning females had levels that might inhibit successful reproduction. These findings correlated well with surveys that disclosed greater numbers of nesting Peregrines and increased nesting success all across the Arctic.

But the bird knew none of this. She knew only that during the days and the miles that stretched back from *this* ledge overlooking *this* bay to *the* ledge overlooking *the* river, she had seen many of her kind, though few had traveled as far as she had. Most of her kin from the Coleville region had moved south along the flank of the Rockies and filtered down along the coast of Mexico. But she had wandered after her family had dissolved during the last part of August. Her course led south, but the large swirling patterns of cold northern air that had tracked high across the continent, system after system, had carried her eastward. The bird could have adjusted her flight to compensate for the gradual drift across the continent, but there seemed to be no reason to do so. Food was plentiful along the route and air was air.

Two days ago, she had left the continent behind and struck out over open water. She was now sufficiently south that her flight passed through the lower portion of the clockwise flow of air. The winds were northeast. After an uncomfortable night aboard the Belegorsk, she had continued south but drifted west with the wind and put in, reluctantly, as darkness overtook her.

Now she was hungry, and it was with the mindfulness of hunger that she probed the world around her. She saw the flicker while it was still several hundred yards from shore. The flicker was exhausted, its energy spent by flight. Several times its weakened undulating flight almost carried it into cresting waves, but it had seen the shore now—and its danger too late.

The Peregrine dropped the updrawn fist of her talons and disclosed for a moment the band that flashed silver in the sun. She roused, muted, and pushed off with the directness of singleminded purpose. She closed quickly on her quarry, reached out with the broad net of her talons, missed the dodging flicker by a shadow's breadth, swung around in a wide arching turn (in typical Peregrine fashion), closed, and did not miss again.

In the south banding station at Cape May Point, New Jersey, Bob Dittrick saw a Peregrine coming in off the Delaware Bay flying heavily, carrying prey. He worked a jacketed lurebird reflexively—once, twice—but without much hope of interesting the bird. He was much too experienced for that. The Peregrine ignored the offering, swung wide of the old concrete bunker where she had spent the night, and took a perch on one of a stand of trees that lay surrounded by open marsh. She attacked her kill in falcon fashion, giving the feathers to the wind.

Releasing the lure line, Bob reached for his binoculars, trained them on the feeding bird, and settled into a comfortable position. Her back was to him and he could not see what kind of prey she had taken. He could only see the tight overlapping mosaic of brown feathers on her back and, when she brought her head up to look around, the dark sideburn-slash on her face and the golden wash of her crown.

"She's a *pretty* young lady," he said aloud in the Virginia-softened syllables that had not been erased by three years of

Alaskan residency. "I'd put a band on that little sweetheart any day she'd say yes."

On her perch, the bird fed hungrily and quickly. She was restless to return to a place that she had never been but would recognize when she got there.

Scotch Bonnet Blind

The old blind sits at the edge of a shallow marsh pond hard by the bay side of Scotch Bonnet Creek. I call it a blind out of a sense of deference because, in truth, nothing remains of the original structure but a gray and weathered frame. It stands, now, stark and silent—silent as the marsh in winter is silent—and both marsh and blind live in the harmony that comes of long familiarity.

The man who built it understood both the marsh and the birds he hunted. There is an understanding of weather and tide about it and how much room a heavily clothed man needs to swing a long-barreled punt gun. There is knowing how to talk in a wary flock of Canadas, how much to lead a Black Duck in a gale, and how a stalking heron will lend an air of well-being to a neatly placed spread of decoys. There is also an understanding and a respect for death woven into the fabric of this blind along with a love for both the marsh and the creatures that live, hunt, and are hunted in it. If a contradiction exists here, I'm sure the man did not see it, and I do not think he would have seen it were it pointed out to him.

The blind is placed high so that only the highest of high tides can reach it. The corner posts are cedar so they will not rot. The cross staves are spiked with copper nails so they will not rust. The pond is large and ringed with tall cordgrass (just right for late-season blacks). It lies close enough to the open bay to tempt a flock of bluebills looking to put in out of foul weather. The blind sits on the landward side facing east because its builder knew that ducks preferred to land into the wind.

It is an old blind but a sturdy one, and the man who built it knew what he was about. I wonder whether he remembers this blind near Scotch Bonnet Creek, and I wonder what his memories are. I wonder how long it has stood there, how many autumns it has seen. I wonder, too, looking at it now, who he was and whether he hunts these marshes still—or other marshes farther afield. I wonder these things because the blind is there even if he is not. Ducks still pitch in before it, not because it is empty, but because the man who built it knew what he was about.

Ducks putting in

A Gift of Vision

His name is Robert Taylor, and he is watching the sky through a pair of binoculars marked "Morristown High School." He starts another scan, low and on the left (just like the High School Hawk Watch manual says), from the goal posts, across the top of the bleachers, past the press box, over B-wing and the cafeteria, and finally across the top of the stately, full-leafed maples that guard the town. Nothing. He doggedly tries it again. Nothing.

Breaking into the Pat Benatar melody running through his mind and some legitimate concerns over an impending test on some boring (and as yet, unread) book called *Pride and Prejudice* is the unwelcome thought that perhaps he is doing something wrong.

Last spring, when Ms. Keller came up from the Cape May Bird Observatory (whatever that is), it had seemed so easy. She had showed them pictures of hawks, lots of them and lots of different kinds. There were Red-tailed Hawks that soared a lot and falcons, like the Peregrine, and even eagles. And they all migrated right over the school. Mrs. Nadolny had said so, too. And so did the manual (so it must be true).

He tried it again—goal posts, bleachers, press box, B-wing . . . and a bird blew through his binocular field startling him half to death. Frantically he swung the glasses back the other way, wildly probing the sky (for a bird that was really only about seventy feet away), and with more luck than skill, found it. He pushed down on the focus lever, lost the bird again as the world melted out of focus, moved it back the other way till the bird became somewhat visible, and began looking for "field marks."

It wasn't a Red-tailed Hawk (that much seemed obvious) and it didn't look big enough for an eagle. (Well, maybe a small eagle.) It had a blue back and it had pointy wings (*pointy wings???*) . . . POINTY WINGS! It was a falcon, one of the really fast ones, and it could be a Peregrine or maybe even a Merlin. (Oh, wouldn't they be impressed if he saw a Peregrine, one of the really rare ones.) But it was going away so he couldn't see the face. (That's how you tell, by looking at the face.) And as he watched, the bird pitched down toward the end zone, landed amidst a group of pigeons, and proceeded to feed.

Hmmmmmmm.

Maybe it was the binoculars, he thought. He looked at the unfamiliar instrument and noticed first of all the big dent on the barrel that he had blackened up with a little magic marker (but it still looked pretty obvious). He moved the focus lever back and forth a few times, twisted the right eyepiece one way, then the other, and brought the binoculars up and held them away from his face (the way Debbie, er, Ms. Keller showed them). This was to check the malignment. *Funny, there doesn't seem to be much light coming through that one side.*

He brought them up to his eyes and focused on the press box, a Coke can, and finally on the cheerleaders who were twisting themselves into impossible positions at the 50-yard line. The binos stayed there a while. For science.

A voice interrupted his field study. "Birdwatcher! Hey, look at the birdwatcher." Two members of the football team had come out to do warm-up laps and as Robert watched, one of them brought his hands up to his eyes in a mocking pantomime and proceeded to look frantically around. He and his friend laughed uproariously at this tremendous display of wit. The cheerleaders were watching too (including Nancy, who sat two desks up and one row over in geometry class).

By all laws governing such social interactions, Robert should have kept quiet. After all, he was a sophomore and they were *seniors.* But planted in him now was the conviction that he was doing something special. The high school hawk watch project wasn't just books and it wasn't just a simulation. It was real, like science. And, besides, Nancy was watching.

"It's not *bird*watching," he said. "It's *hawk* watching. They're different." Robert couldn't exactly explain *why* they were different; he just knew that they were.

But the young gladiators didn't answer; perhaps they didn't even hear him. They had realized that they were approaching the cheerleaders and had broken into a brisk stride.

The outside bell sounded, posting notice that the period had ended. He had ten minutes to get to class. His relief would be here soon.

Robert tried it again. Goal posts, bleachers, press box, B-wing, . . . goal posts, bleachers, press box, B-wing . . . and again. He was beginning to get a headache.

He heard the measured thumps of someone climbing the bleachers just as the five-minute bell sounded. It was Susan. She was on the staff of the literary magazine and wanted to be a poet. She said she had joined the hawk watch to "broaden her awareness."

"Did you see any?" she asked hopefully. "Hawks?" she added quickly. (Susan liked to be precise.)

"Well, I might have seen a Peregrine," Robert said (not lying very much). "But it might have been something else. It was pretty far," he added (lying just a little bit more).

Quickly he turned over the binoculars and the "Hawk Watch Attack Pack" (clipboard, thermometer, HMANA daily report forms, raptor I.D. chart, hawk watch instruction book, and an assortment of gum wrappers and stale-dated late passes lying at the bottom of the canvas bag). Susan donned the binoculars, adjusted the individual eyepiece to precisely $+1\frac{1}{2}$ and proceeded to scan . . . goal posts, bleachers, press box . . .

Robert headed for the main building before she noticed the dent. He crossed the cinder track at a run, using the long, fluid strides of a born 880 man—something the track coach had not failed to notice last spring. He crossed the football field, only slowing to a walk when he reached the blacktop parking lot rippling with heat in the afternoon sun.

"What am I doing wrong!" They had been watching for five days now and aside from the few birds seen on the first day when they had been out with Ms. Keller, nobody had seen a hawk. It had been really hot for September. Maybe that had something to do with it. He knew from the guide that hawks flew best when it was cold. Or maybe the hawks were flying too high to be seen or they just didn't fly over Morristown. Or maybe, he thought, finally confronting the unwelcome possibility, maybe since he got headaches, he wasn't doing it right.

He didn't see the stubby little buteo that came in low over B-wing and caught the thermal off the hot macadam lot. He didn't see it, in fact, until it had been joined by two others. And it wasn't until they were joined by a fourth bird, showing two dark bands on the tail, that he realized what was happening.

They're hawks, his mind said, pushing all doubt before it. *They're hawks. Like the ones in the slide—Broad-tails or something. The ones that fly all the way to South America. Broad-tails!*

He willed his eyes away from the sky and shouted toward Susan. He waved both arms and shouted again, but it was no good. It was too far. Susan seemed to be having difficulty with the binoculars and she wasn't looking.

Robert gave himself up to watching. He didn't look for field marks, wing molt, or crop size. He didn't even look to see if they were adults or immatures. He just looked at the birds, the way they swirled hypnotically within the invisible ball of rising air until they were just sparks of sunlight against sky. He watched the way they streamed away, how the group of birds just got smaller and smaller and disappeared, and how the sky didn't look empty after the last birds had drifted from sight. In fact, the sky was richer than it had ever been before.

The buzzer sounded and he sprinted the remaining fifty yards to the door. It wasn't until he reached the steps that he remembered. He looked back at the football field. The cheerleaders were taking a break, and he was pretty sure that one of them was watching him.

Her name is Ann Van Sweringen and she is watching the sky through three inches of sunlight that is the viewing slit for the east banding station. If you were close enough to see her clearly, you would find a young face, a woman's face neatly framed by brown hair cut short for ease. Her eyes are a deep, somber brown—intelligent and alert. If you failed to see the intensity in her eyes, you could not help but see it mapped across her face. Ann is a skilled biologist and a hawk bander, a member of a very small and very select group. More than this, she is a Peregrine bander, of an elite caste within the order of hawk banders.

But you would have to be very close to see all of these things, and you would have to be in the station itself to see her mastery of her trade—how her hand knows the way to several lure lines (leaving her eyes free to watch the skies). The way she keeps her face away from the viewing slit (so it does not catch the sun) or the way the blind is arranged, with every piece of equipment arrayed precisely for ease.

Radiating out from the blind, like battlefield telephone lines from a command center, are the lure lines. Each runs toward a short-cut post and then down to a snap swivel riveted to a tough, protective leather jacket. Encased in the jackets are Ann's teammates, specialists in their own right—lurebirds.

Out front, bold as brass, is Goliath—reputed to be the best flapper pigeon in Cape May. Goliath's job is to catch the attention of passing Peregrines. To his right, down in the trenches, is Spike, a grizzled, bull starling (who hasn't met the Sharp-shinned Hawk he couldn't lick). Spike's job is to entice young or timid (or male) Peregrines, the ones that take one look at Goliath and decide to bolt. On the left, taking some sun in front of her protective shed, is Molly, the seductive House Sparrow promising earthly delights for the small price of a band.

Around the station, placed so strategically that only an experienced bander could appreciate their genius, are several nets. Most banding stations are shot through with nets—mist nets, dho-ghaza nets, bow nets—so that the terrain in front of a typical banding station looks like the rigging of a clipper ship on washday. But Ann's station is different.

Peregrines are birds of the open and they harbor an immense dislike for clutter. A typical banding station would intimidate a Peregrine, so Ann's is a study in space and utilitarian design. The nets are spare and set precisely where a Peregrine's course should carry it. The probability of capture is equal to the number of nets (N) plus the number of passes (P) divided by the difference between the inexperience of the bird (I) and the experience of the bander (E). By this equation, Ann's station is a Nobel prize-winner, but there is one other key factor at play here. It might or might not be the most determining but it is the most elusive—"luck." So far, this element had played against Ann and her stationmates.

Three Peregrines had challenged her station and three birds had eluded capture, two of them after lengthy, arm-aching, throat-catching, heart-pumping duels. After four days of operation, Ann's stringer of Lock-on No. 7 bands still held fifty.

If Ann had not forgotten the birds that got away, neither did she dwell on them. After the most recent frustrating match, she had stepped back and cast an appraising eye over her station, removed one dho-ghaza from behind Spike (she decided it was in the way), moved one mist net two feet closer, fine-tuned the trigger on her main bow net, and added some more camouflage to the blind. It was early in the season and the time for modifications was now. Later there would be no time.

Ann reached for her binoculars and mapped a careful search of the sky. Nothing. She studied each of her lure birds in turn and looked for signs of fatigue. They looked fine. Grasping the main line, she gave a hefty tug, launching Goliath. He fluttered indignantly to earth and then did a solo sortie of his own (just to cement the understanding that *he* knew his business). Ann smiled, satisfied, and turned her eyes back to the sky over Cape May. Her mind, unfettered of concerns, turned in upon itself

113

and released the musings and memories that are the constant companion of biologists who spend long periods in the field alone.

"Hawk watch to East."

Part of Ann's mind reached back to the present as her hand reached for the radio. "Go ahead hawk watch," she said, completing the litany.

"Ann, we just had a bird off to the north and wondered if maybe you saw it?"

She knew without asking that "bird" meant Peregrine, but couched as it was in ambiguity, it meant that either Harry wasn't sure about the identification or, out of deference, didn't want to imply that she had missed something.

"No, Harry, I didn't see anything unusual (*I didn't see a Peregrine*). There's been a harrier working the meadows all morning, though (*Could you have mistaken a harrier for a Peregrine?*).

"Weeeelll, it might have been just a harrier," Harry replied. "It was kinda up and down and far away. It *might* have been just a harrier but it might have been something else though," he added, not wanting to actually say the name.

"Well, OK. Thanks for the tip," Ann replied. "I'll keep my eyes open," she added (not wanting to say the name, either, because sometimes if you want something badly and you say it, it will not happen).

"East clear."

"Hawkwatchout."

Ann replaced the radio and returned her attention to the viewing slit. The Peregrine was fifty yards out, two feet off the ground, and closing.

Molly chirped a warning and made a dive for her shelter. Spike crouched low, doing his best imitation of a dirt ball. Ann hit the main lure line, letting Goliath fly in a wide arch and then settle. The Peregrine came in fast, pulling up at just the last second to take her quarry as it flushed. Goliath merely ducked. He had played this game before.

The Peregrine overshot Goliath badly and barely missed the top of a mist net. Surprised by Goliath's breach of etiquette,

It wasn't just a harrier. . . it was something else.

the falcon took longer than usual to complete her turn—the wide, sweeping turn of a tundra Peregrine.

Ann hit the lure line again, giving Goliath some rope. The Peregrine closed again, pulled up, missed (barely clearing another net, turned, closed, and missed—again, and then again.

The young falcon took her time about coming in now. She knew where the nets were, and though she didn't recognize their purpose, she knew them as obstacles to be avoided. She didn't like the way they interfered with her attacks and she didn't like the way this strange bird acted (in fact, there were a lot of things that she didn't like about this whole situation). When she came in this time, there was just a little less urgency in her flight, a caution that edged very close to disinterest.

Ann sensed, rather than saw, the change in the bird. A plan crystalized in her mind. It was unorthodox and if she had just a little more time to think about it, she probably would have dismissed it as unworkable.

Releasing Goliath, Ann took a deep breath and brought Spike into the arena with two quick tugs of the line. The Peregrine veered, accelerating toward the new target. Just as she pulled up, Ann shouted loud enough to make her ears ring.

"HEY!"

Startled, the Peregrine veered sharply away from the blind, veered when she should have climbed, and then belonged to the net.

His name is Frank Schleicher and he is watching the sky, part of the river, the top of the ridge, and a small, insignificant, and all-important dot through the viewfinder of a Canon Fl camera. The dot was still a good three minutes upridge, but there was no question that it was an eagle.

When Frank had first picked up the bird, it was far more likely to be overlooked than misidentified. Only someone who had looked up that ridge a hundred thousand times *could* have seen it, someone who knew every curve and hollow of the ridge, every limb and outcropping.

But how this small, dark pinhole in an ice-blue sky could possibly be identified at this distance is even harder to define. Maybe it had something to do with the darkness of the object, so dark that distance and bright sunlight could not mask it. Maybe it was a matter of *bearing*, the way it came down the ridge steadily, straying from the contours of the ridgetop no more than a train from its track (this is how an eagle signs its name).

But the truth is that Frank made it an eagle at this distance. The myriad of subjective hints and clues that poured out from the bird were filtered through the mesh of a hawkwatcher's mind. Charged particles of fact linked up with mirror images held fast in experience. Their sum, taken together, formed a composite reality, a Golden Eagle.

The 400mm lens bounced slightly, in measure with each contraction of Frank's heart (heartbeats that could not be attributed to the climb to the top). He had been there long enough to find his wind, long enough to feel the chill of Canadian air as it probed for weak points through the armor of wool. Long enough, in fact, to have given thought to taking a quick run to get warm. But he wasn't cold now.

He had reached the top just a little after 9 AM and he had noted with measures of pride that even at age 65, he could still make it to the crest in something under thirty minutes. He had felt anxious all the way up—he could not discern the wind. *But that is to be expected*, he kept reminding himself. *This is the second day after the front. The winds will be lighter and I won't feel them until I clear the top.*

As he neared the crest, long past the time that the welcome tightness in his calves had become a familiar ache and finally an agony, he heard the reassuring rattle of branches exposed to the wind. The crest fell away to reveal a broad valley that swept north until it broke against the foothills of the Poconos. To the south lay the rolling farmland of northwestern New Jersey. Running north and east were the serpentine contours of the Kittatinny Ridge.

As he rested, Frank recalled yesterday's flight. The first real cold front in two weeks had passed through, timed perfectly to catch the peak of the Red-tailed migration. The birds had responded beautifully—several hundred Red-taileds, a number of Red-shouldereds, a late Osprey, an early Rough-legged, and a Gos (*Oh, that dirty, sneaking Gos!*) that had made pass after murderous pass at the owl decoy just as Frank was changing film.

Frank had burned two full rolls and was pretty sure that there would be one or two quality shots. Most photographers would kill for some of the photos that Frank threw away, but Frank was a perfectionist—an artist—and only the very best were kept and these he circulated for nothing. He was retired now. Money had ceased to be a concern. Photographing hawks was something that gave him pleasure, and mixing photography up with money would only diminish that feeling. So he gave his shots away to organizations he favored—and there were many.

In less than five minutes he was at *his* spot, a little way downridge and just off the trail. In ten minutes more, his trusty, battle-scarred owl decoy was in place, his camera loaded, the settings checked, and his thermos in easy reach. Frank was a veteran campaigner and this was his tenth season at this site.

Birds were just starting to get up out of the trees down in the valleys. It would take them a while to get up to the ridge. Frank watched through his binoculars as two widely spaced Red-taileds rose slowly off to the northeast. They mantled their fragile columns of rising air, the first thermals of the morning. First one bird, then the other made for the ridge and its energy-conserving updraft. That was when he saw the incredibly distant, indescribably dark bird upridge at the limit of conjecture. The Red-taileds were forgotten. . . .

The lens bounced slightly, but with the camera mounted on a shoulder stock and with a shutter speed of 1/500 of a second, it would be all right. He mentally rechecked his settings (trying to recall whether he had remembered to move the exposure compensation dial back to zero after taking those scenery shots on the way up) and tried not to think of all the little things that could go wrong.

He must have spent the night on the ridge, he thought. *I don't think he could have gotten up to the ridge from down in the valley this early. But you never know. No, you never know with eagles.*

He heard, so close it startled him, a sound like a sharply drawn breath and he knew that one of the Red-taileds had stooped on the owl decoy. Frank did not turn his head. He did not move at all, because it was certain that the eagle had noted the Red-tailed's stoop as well and that those incredible eyes that have no concept of distance were turned on him now.

Will this bird come in on the owl, he wondered. *It almost never happens.*

As if to answer, the bird slid closer to the ridge, against the dark backdrop of trees. Unless you knew precisely where to look, the bird was invisible. But through the lens it was close enough now to see the small white patches bleeding through the top of the wings and the stark, white tail rimmed by a broad, dark band.

A young bird, a part of his mind recorded gratefully. *Inexperienced*, another part echoed. The bird dropped lower now, below the treetops that would cover its approach.

He's coming in, his mind said, finally accepting it.

"Good Lord, he's coming in," Frank said softly to himself as he shifted slightly into a position that eased some of the tension that was building in his arms. That was when he heard the sound that brought the hollow-sick feeling to his stomach—the sound of someone walking heavily up the trail.

A backpacker, he thought, and in his mind he could picture the figure behind him decked out in all the psychotropic, petroleum-based gear that makes its wearer about as inconspicuous as a shell-burst. But it would be the motion that would kill everything—the thumping, long strides, the widely swinging arms, the pack, swinging side to side like the hindquarters of a mule. The eagle, no matter how inexperienced, would see the moving figure as soon as it cleared the trees and that would be the end of that.

Frank took a deep breath and said just loud enough to be heard over the thump of boots, "Listen, whoever you are, please don't move." The thumping stopped. "There's an eagle coming in so please just wait a minute," he added.

The person, whoever it was, did not answer—but did not move, either.

Nothing happened for ten, then twenty, then thirty seconds. Anxiety began to gnaw deeper into Frank's mind. He knew that the backpacker must be getting impatient and might not even have believed him. *Who'd believe anyone who said that there was an eagle flying by?*

He was all set to offer additional reassurance when the bird cleared the trees. "Here he comes," he said softly, and then he concentrated all of his being on the bird.

It was close, and through the viewfinder it looked massive. Frank had prepared himself for this, but after Red-taileds, the size of the bird through the viewfinder was staggering. He didn't wait for the bird to reach the owl; he didn't need to—the bird almost filled the frame already. Frank took two deep breaths, let the last one halfway out, focused on the head of the bird, and touched the shutter release.

Kajeet, the motor drive whined. He focused again, making sure each wing tip was in the field . . . *Kajeet*.

Maybe a hair off on that one, he thought, focusing a bit more.

Kajeet . . . Kajeet . . .

The bird pulled up, sensing for the first time that something was not as it should be.

Kajeet.

The bird turned its head, pinned its gaze to the source of the sound and took in the figure.

Kajeet.

The bird flared and drew away from the ridge with deep, pushing wingbeats. It looked back once, more curious than alarmed, and drew gradually away.

Frank relaxed, letting out the long-held breath and gratefully drawing in another. He turned to thank the backpacker for his patience and looked full into the face of a young woman wearing a faded plaid jacket and an expression like she had just witnessed a miracle.

And maybe she had at that, Frank mused. *If one of those shots turns out, I'll bet she'd like a print.*

His name is Maurice Broun and once he watched the skies over Hawk Mountain, Pennsylvania. His eyes are closed, now, but he watches, still, through the eyes that he gave to others—a marvelous gift of vision that has touched the life of every hawkwatcher who has ever faced into an autumn sky.

Not a hawk is seen, not an identification made, that Maurice doesn't figure into it. And the magic of this gift is such that through our eyes, Maurice Broun is immortal (no less than he deserves).

A gift of vision looks both ways. It looks back to a lone pioneer standing on a rocky outcropping fifty years ago; it looks out from the bleachers on a football field, in the eyes of a boy . . .

His name is Robert Taylor, and he is watching the sky through a pair of binoculars marked "Morristown High School."

A Confederate Hawkwatcher from AK-625

The radar screen glowed soft and empty at Raptor Recording Station AK-625. Weather control satellites were not due to push the cold front through until 1130 hours, two hours later than scheduled to reduce chances of rain falling on the V-ME Day parade in *New* New York. The small group of Guild Raptor Recorders lounged comfortably, ran lens tissues over the readout panels of their pocket flight analyzers, and passed the time with small talk and premature lunches.

The old man stared through the plexiglass weather dome overhead. He often did that.

AK-625 is rated AAA in the twenty-second rework of *The Guide to Raptor Recording Stations North of Tierra del Fuego*. It is perched on the rim of the Salem Crater, a geological formation formed back in the last century when some cranky old nuke plant scored a meltdown and ionized most of the old states of Delaware, Pennsylvania, and New Jersey (and drove Cape May clear through the island of Bermuda). Northwest winds set up a creditable updraft along its three thousand foot rim. (What you may have heard about the place being so "hot" that it sets up thermals at midnight is simply unsubstantiated.) Raptor migration recordings have been conducted at several points along the rim since it was ruled "lukenuke" a dozen years ago.

Talk turned, as it always does at RR outposts, to flights, faces, and places of bygone days. Shop talk. All the greats were mentioned: Derby Hill, New York, and the spring flight of 1983; Bridger Mountain, Montana, and the one thousand

122

Golden Eagle autumn; Holiday Beach, Ontario, and the hundred thousand Broad-winged day; the Goshawk invasion of Hawk Ridge in 2012; and the Peregrine incursion at Padre Island, Texas, in '98. But by and by someone said, "Well, none of 'em could hold a candle to Cape May if half of what you hear is true," and the room fell into silence as the first few raindrops dotted the protective dome.

The flights at Cape May, New Jersey, were legendary, and some of the younger Guild Recorders just flat out didn't believe them. One young JG, fresh out of Wind Gap Training Center, rushed into an erudite discourse on the "Piltdown Effect," a thesis often attributed to Oscar Huff of Back Burner Knob, who is said to have discovered a correlation between Cape May figures and Cheerios spilled on his kitchen counter ($r = 0.06 \ldots$ sometimes).

The kid was just warming to the subject when a single, terse expletive at the edge of the group cut him short. Heads turned to find Pops, the veteran, regarding them with an expression that was partly amusement, but partly something that wasn't.

The group settled back in their chairs because Pops could spin a rare tale when he had a mind to. It was rumored that he used to watch hawks through twin-barreled vision amplifiers and that he was a card-carrying member of the outlawed, underground "weathermen" branch of the disbanded Hawk Migration Association of North America. There was no denying his long years of service. One look at him dispelled any doubt. Pop's head was permanently drawn back, an occupational deformity called "hawkwatcher's neck." It was caused by the incalculable hours spent peering upward through the old magnidomes. In those days, migrating hawks were identified using the ancient art of "flight identification."

The youngster brashly maintained the offensive and advanced a textbook defense of Piltdown. A sharp look from Pops stopped him cold.

"Don't hand me any of that tripe ya double-counting young pup. I was watching hawks long before you was a drain on the social revenue banks." Pops spat skillfully in the direction of the UNITRACK TC-2000 Raptoranalyzer (standard issue since

2058), gazed thoughtfully at the vacant radar screen, and started his tale.

"I was there in October of 1979," he said. *"There,* I tell ya. Fresh outa college with a spankin' new degree in Wildlife Management and nuthin' but time to kill. Jes' about your age," he added, gesturing toward the young JG. "Young fella name 'a Dowdell manning the *hawk watch* (Pops always used the old terms) and 'nuther fella fillin' in now'n ag'in . . . ferget his name, now.

"Well, I gets there on the first. A no-account flight with a couple a Peregrines and a dozen Merlin." He paused here. "They was *life* birds for me then. Only a couple hundred birds all day and talk around the watch was about how it was fixin' to be an average year." He chuckled softly, looked long and hard at the radar screen, and repeated, "An average year.

"It was southwest and slow off the line on the morning of the second—maybe a hundred birds passed afore 0900. Then, jes' like that, things catch fire and we're into Peregrines likc someone opened the gates to the mews o'heaven. Twenty-one for the day," he said with a nod, "twenty-one."

The young JG whipped out his pocket flighta'lizer and tapped a complicated series of codes into: "Historic Recall." "Twenty-one is the officially recognized total *barring* any duplication."

Pops straightened up like he was stung, and if looks could dispatch, the JG would have been waltzing with the cosmic. But before he could retort, someone else asked—"Say, wasn't that the day the Godfather died?" And while the kid hit the appropriate buttons for "Recall, Famous Hawk Watchers," Pops sort of crumbled into his chair wearing a look of pure shock that turned slowly into a wide grin.

"Yeah," he said, turning back to the group, "yeah, that was the day all right. You know, I never put it together like that before." But he didn't elaborate, and whatever it was that he was thinking he kept to himself.

"Well, anyway," he continued, "hawks started pourin' through the Cape from that time on. Two and three thousand a day on the average. Mostly Sharpies o' course but Peregrines, *good Gyr*, Peregrines, ten or twenty a day for over a week and Merlins! Merlins jest cuttin' through the *Phragmites* like lasers through cheese makin' life miserable fer the dicky birds."

A tap of fingers on keys was followed by a voice loud with triumph: "One hundred and twenty-nine Merlins on 6 October, a decade record, and 265 Ospreys on the ninth, standing record for the most Ospreys ever recorded in one hawk watch standard."

Pops continued. "Hell's jesses, falcons jes' about run things till midmonth. Then it rains on the fourteenth or fifteenth . . ."

"The thirteenth," pipes the computer's accomplice.

"Yeah, the thirteenth," Pops muses. "They was 185 P-birds seen that month. Check me on that," he said. (The kid nods.) "And seven or eight hundred Merlins."

"Seven hundred and seventy-eight," echos the keeper of the keys.

"But next day, all hell breaks loose and Dowdell is durn near strippin' the gears on his clickers trying to keep up with the flight. Sharpies and kestrels pourin' through like winter was snappin' at their subterminals. Almost 8,000 that day. Make a good season's worth now," he added softly.

"What's *winter*?" somebody whispered.

"Shut up," suggested somebody else. "The man's talkin'."

"The rain changed the whole timbre o' the fall it seemed to me. Falcons dwindled; buteos and accipiters took up the slack. Cooper's was as thick as Democratic contenders after a Republican administration. They was a hundred Cooper's a day on the average for the rest o' the month. And 347 on 18 October alone."

He chuckled here. "Took a lot of grief for *that* figure you can bet, but Cooper's was up all over that year. Last big migration ever recorded I recollect."

"What's a Cooper's?" a faceless voice inquired.

"Cooper's *Hawk*," another voice snapped. "Subspecies of Sharp-shinned, *Accipiter striatus cooperii*. Lumped 'em back in '21. Shhhhh!"

"They was lots o' other good days," Pops continued, "but I ferget a lot, now. It was a long time ago. Four Golden Eagles and one Bald on the twenty-seventh, three more Goldens on the twenty-ninth, and a Ferruginous Hawk was seen by one of the network hawk watches."

Pops didn't say anything for a while. His eyes were closed and he looked as if he'd drifted off to sleep. Some of the group began to stir uneasily in their chairs.

Pops opened his eyes and continued, slowly, and with a hint of something that might have been sadness. "I had to leave on the twenty-ninth for a job interview on the West Coast, but Dowdell sent me the results when they got 'em all compiled. Nice fella, Dowdell.

"They was 60,307 hawks seen that month. Check me if you like. I never got to go back," he added after a short pause. "Sorry, now."

The room fell into silence.

"Hey," one of the group shouted, "I got a bird—17.4km and closing!"

All eyes turned to the radar screen and the small green dot on the outer edge of the northeast quadrant. Coordinates were quickly punched into the Unitrack and a sensor beam locked on target.

"Small accipiter for my money," said one fellow. "Makin' 2.3 . . . no, .4 wingbeats per second with an atmospheric compensation factor of 0.0110."

"Don't be a jerk," countered another and more experienced RR Tech person. "Look at that wing-loading datum. Falls squarely in the falcon range. Kestrel most likely—beating quickly 'cause its still wet. But, the Unitrack should have a positive ID in a second or two."

The old man hadn't moved. The crick in his neck made it look as if he were peering at the cumulus clouds whipping silently over the weather dome.

But then, he often did that.

Shearwater Sunday

We steer for Orion's belt. Venus smiles coldly to port; Taurus looks on, stupid or impassive, to starboard. I am watching, too, from the deck behind the bridge, with my feet planted stubbornly against the sea—(but one hand firmly on the rail for insurance).

Shooting stars arch overhead. Five for the hour on northwest winds, a good count for so late in the season. Perhaps they are a sign for a good day's birding from some benign god. But I'm a birder, not an oracle, and if stars portend the future, they are beyond my skill to interpret. Besides, nobody *gives* information away anymore. It's a commodity, bought and sold.

The world, to an unbroken horizon, lies in darkness. Land is an hour at twelve knots in the *Big Jim*'s wake. Strewn along the length of the ship are eighty-odd members of the New Jersey birding community. Some sleep, some pretend to. Some gather in tight clusters, knotted by friendship. And some stand silently alone, sending thoughts probing eternity.

Few with lines anchored in sanity are comfortable with the world that lies on the dark side of dawn. Old, familiar habits are cut loose from their moorings and set adrift in the gray seas that separate two worlds. Day things and night things mingle side by side, and the sounds they produce give rise to the most half-cracked orchestration this side of order. The scrape of a Stanley thermos being opened is punctuated by the snap of a Budweiser pull tab. Dull snores mix with sharp laughter, mingle with the sizzle of burgers and hash browns on the grill, and are swept toward heaven on the roar of diesel engines. Lunacy.

Greater Shearwater—cutting the surface like a knife

The sky brightens without color and the rails on both sides of the ship begin to fill with shapes and faces taut with watchfulness. Someone near the stern shouts something that is taken and scattered by the wind as he gestures into the darkness. Others take up hue and cry. Eager faces strain forward.

Three slim, dark forms emerge from the spray thrown from

128

the ship's bow. Shadows without sunlight, they pace the ship for a time before drifting from sight.

Questions file down the line of observers.

"What were they? Anybody get an ID on 'em? What's the consensus?"

An answer files back, "Sooty Shearwaters, they say."

"Yeah, who's 'they'? All shearwaters look sooty in the dark."

Another shout goes up. Three large shearwaters lift off the water as Captain Dulinski cuts the engines. Alan Brady digs a ladle deep into a garbage can whose contents might best be likened to a nightmare held in suspension—ground menhaden in natural brine, a gastronomic abomination. The oil-impregnated stew spreads a slick that widens with each swell. One bird turns to investigate, then another, sweeping in as silent as owls in falling snow.

Neophytes to *steep water* birding work out identifications point by point. *Largish shearwater . . . dark-backed . . . light underparts . . . dark-rumped . . . indistinct line between the face and cap . . . too dark to see the bill color.*

Veterans do it in flash uptake, saltwater gestalt.

Bull-headed shearwater. Cory's!

Captain Dulinski, eyes like glacial melt, watches from the door to the cabin, taking it all in. Birders are a new phenomenon to him. Forty years on party boats have given him a seaman's savvy that you would have to search long and hard to equal. He knows fish and he knows fishermen and, in a fisherman's sort of way, he knows birds, too. He knows that when you find fish, you generally find birds. But birders are a new phenomenon and his interest is piqued, just as it had been by the mysteries of biology that had held his fascination as a premed student years earlier. Lack of experience notwithstanding, the captain knows when customers are pleased, and if his eyes aren't deceiving him, his eighty customers are mighty pleased at the moment.

Other shearwaters are sighted in the wake of a scalloper, a seagoing shellfish enterprise that sees a small part of an animal utilized and one heck of a lot of shellfish thrown to the gulls (or the bottom). More chum is ladled out. The scalloper's feathered satellites respond like children to the arrival of an ice cream truck.

A Greater Shearwater sweeps up from the rim of a trough and banks softly left, his wing cutting the glassy, windless sea like a knife—*shearing* the water.

Cory's and Greaters sweep around the boat in a gentle frenzy. And then they are gone, in singles and pairs, disappearing into troughs and morning sunlight, leaving only held breaths and an empty ocean to mark their passage.

The captain misses nothing. If the school moves out and they stop hitting the bait, move on! The *Big Jim*'s twin diesels rumble to life and the ship leans forward.

The engines throttle down to idle and in answer to the unvoiced quesion, the loudspeaker on the bridge touts: "Baltimore Canyon, end of the line."

"Everybody out," somebody quips—predictably.

The *Jim* rocks gently in the swells and sargasso weed. Eighty pairs of binoculars sweep three-hundred and sixty degrees of ocean.

No birds.

We spread a chum slick so broad you'd swear the Italian sardine fleet had wrecked. But aside from a handful of Wilson's Petrels and the marlin fleet, the ocean is empty.

On the port side, a fivesome of keen, albeit inattentive-eyed birders stare vacantly into space. Pete Bacinski, Frank Frazier, Clay Sutton, Bob Russell, and me. Eyestrain, a shortage of sleep, and the lulling sounds of mother sea have combined to enchant us into a state that might pass for sleep in a group composed of less formidable birders. High-geared attentiveness notwithstanding, the dinky little (small "l") shearwater manages to sneak up awfully close before it attracts a mild form of attention, an attention that widens in quanta of one jump per heartbeat.

The bird is smallish, the dorsal surface is uniformly dark, the cap is indented just behind the eye (giving the bird the slightest suggestion of a sideburn). The tail is longish and dark below;

the wings are slightly rounded, and the wingbeats are quick and steady. *And,* it is a life bird for five out of five. Audubon's Shearwaters are not stock items for New Jersey birders.

It happens so fast that it's almost too late to call the attention of the rest of the group to the quickly receding bird, although we try (and they do, too). Only a handful of the party manages to catch a glimpse of the bird. So it goes with pelagic birding—or any birding for that matter.

On the return trip, curious to hear his thoughts, I sidle up to Captain Dulinski.

"Captain, I've been associating with birders for so long that they seem about as ordinary as nine-to-five. Now that you've seen them in action, what do you think of them?"

The captain moves his eyes carefully over the deck and weighs his words.

"They're an all-right bunch. And intense! I've never seen people so interested in anything they were doing. Now take fishermen. If it gets toward midmorning and the fish stop hitting, they drop their poles, reach for a beer, and bellyache. Just look at these birders," he adds, shaking his head in admiration. "I've never seen people more interested in what they were doing."

And I'm inclined to agree with the captain—but then, I'm not in a position to be objective.

Death of a Season

There were auguries that maybe only the wise could read, several days before summer died. A tern was seen with a black teardrop etched over its eyes and the Yankees broke a nine-game losing streak (beating the Indians eight to five). Lines of pelicans appeared over beach bathers and there was great wonder. At the C-View Inn, regular patrons had to wait for a table. The price of strawberries went up forty cents and blueberries were offered for a dollar. Asparagus had vanished.

At the Second Avenue jetty, a pretty, young housewife screamed: "Damn kid . . . yer out too far! Tommy, what did I tell you? Get in here! Get in here this instant!!!"

And he did, too.

There were these signs and others. It should have come as no surprise. The death of a season does not come unheralded.

I went to South Cape May "to stretch my legs," I told others.

"To see what was around," I lied to myself.

But the truth was, I went to witness. Just because miracles weren't in vogue this summer doesn't mean that a stone should roll back from a tomb or a tree should fall in a forest without a witness.

What good are blueberries at a buck even if nobody buys them?

I parked my car on Sunset, grabbed my binoculars (the honored badge of my order) and my blueberries, found the gate latched (Wilson, Darwin, Audubon be praised, another miracle), unlatched it, rehooked it, and moved south through the meadows. My eyes were fixed on the sky. The sign would surely come from there. All the real good ones do, anyway.

Portents were never better. Three days had passed since midsummer's eve (and three is a sure-fire figure where augury is concerned). The angle of the sun was proved perfect, and to top things off, the season's first cold front had slipped through during the dark hours before dawn.

It passed without heat lightning or the rumbles of thunder that send homeowners scampering to windows. It came silently, unnoticed except by the stars that blazed brighter in welcome, the curtains in west-facing windows, and the vigilant house cats (which have never let a curtain stir unseen since they traded the night sky for the hearth).

It was late and I hurried. Already the sun was melting the shadows. The cattle had retreated to the refuge of the trees. The Least Terns crouched low in the sand.

On the hill, at midpoint, I scanned the grassy flats and searched the rippled pools. I would accept only a dowitcher or a Lesser Yellowlegs, I had decided. Plovers were risky harbingers for something as serious as the death of a season. And peep were treacherous. You could *never* be sure which way a Least Sandpiper was heading in June—never. Just yesterday, a flock of three Westerns, one Semipalmated, two Leasts, and a White-rumped Sandpiper had touched down. The White-rumped had to be a spring leftover; probably the Westerns and Semi as well. But the Least was a toss-up—northbound or southbound, heads or tails (call it in the air). But justice prevailed. They left, flying north, revealing themselves at last— lollers and spring leftovers.

No, peep make poor prophets.

The meadows were wavy with heat. The sand hurt the eyes to look at it. Beyond the dunes, polyester-girded beach people were having a spirited game of Frisbee. Beyond the wind-sharpened breakers, the Hobie Cats cut back and forth in a melee of rainbow colors.

It was summer over there, just a scant mile away.

Horned Lark on the meadows

And it was still summer in the meadows, too. The usual assemblage of molt-masked puddle ducks lounged off to the right. A full scan produced a half-dozen Killdeer, two ratty-looking Black-bellied Plovers, and the three Greater Yellowlegs that had been here since May. Nothing had changed. I wasn't too late.

The activity on the beach was daunting. Summer seemed so real and so close; but I was not fooled. I come from a long line of Druids. My ancestors communicated with the wind and the sun before they learned speech. I am not of the Frisbee and the Hobie Cat; my faith is not compromised by the frozen daiquiri. I waited.

Summer died quickly this year. Why, it was hardly any vigil at all. Indecision would have served as well. Maybe it just comes of having faith and knowing the signs.

The bird called behind and close at hand.

Tu, tu. Tu, tu, tu.

The dowitcher dropped rapidly, spilling wind from its wings, then accelerated and sped by, showing the full orange color of its breast and the white token of identification on its back. It

Dowitchers heading south

circled twice, then headed south, still calling. It would have been more auspicious if the bird had landed, but, well, you take your miracles where you find them.

The Willets stood with sheathed beaks. Their time was coming. In less than a week, they would follow the dowitcher south. It has always been this way.

Tommy stopped paddling when he reached the end of the jetty. He waited for his mother to yell again. She didn't. He let his hands drift alongside the float, watched the way his arms bent without pain where they entered the water, and chanced a look back toward the beach. His mom was talking to the nice young lifeguard who had let Tommy sit on his stand yesterday. She wasn't paying any attention to him at all.

He stayed out another five minutes. He would have stayed longer but the wind was cold and there weren't any waves.

A bird went by, calling softly.

Sitkagi Spring

On my desk, next to the typewriter, is a stone. Except for the fact that it is the only stone here, there is little to distinguish it from any number of other stones. It would probably elicit different thoughts in different people. A contractor would look at it as a good base for a roadbed and wish he had a billion of them; he would see dollar signs. A geologist would see granite worn smooth by the action of ocean or stream; he would see a story. A crib-bound toddler might merely see "pretty"—but then again, maybe not. It really isn't a pretty stone. But to my mind, aside from the memory of the place it unlocks, the stone is a skipper, and a beauty, too.

If your years are long or your mind too corroded with grown-up cares to recall what a skipper is, I'll remind you. A skipper is a special work of nature designed to dance across the surface of lakes and rivers—and bays, providing your heart is in it and your aim is true. Not just any old rock will do. It takes an awful lot to make a good skipper.

The stone must be about four sticks of gum wide and round as a cat's-eye agate. It has to be small enough so your pointer finger and thumb encircle it, but not so small that fingertip and thumb touch. If they do, it's too small and you can't make it spin right. It has to feel good in your hand, so good that you'll hold it long, savoring its perfection and feeling its potency. So good that you aren't sure whether to throw it or put it in your pocket. To keep.

I owe my knowledge of skippers to a boyhood spent near Bee Meadow Pond. Good skippers were rare. Several generations of

Peregrine head-on

European descendants (and Lord knows how many Lenape youths) had scoured the banks clean of quality skippers. Sometimes I searched from after school right up to dinner and found nothing but shale and skipper seconds.

But on my desk is a skipper, a beauty, one of the best that I have ever seen. I took it from a beach called Sitkagi, which lies a continent away. I took it from a beach whose edge was paved with classic skippers, a beach bordered by the Gulf of Alaska on one side and a small glacier the size of Rhode Island on the other—where whales swim a skipper's toss away, harriers pass overhead, and the sound of Trumpeter Swans filters through the Sitka Spruce. I picked it up, but I didn't throw it. I put it in my pocket, so it could sit on my desk at Cape May for a time . . . so I could write this story.

I climbed through layers of consciousness slowly, letting the world take hold gradually. The first thing I realized was that I was cold; the second, that I had been cold all night; the third, that there was some sort of precipitation hitting the fly of our tent. I learned, as the days slipped one into another, how to judge weather by that sound. A steady patter meant rain. An intermittent patter meant that the rain had stopped. A loud PLOP—SCRAPE meant wet snow falling from boughs a hundred feet overhead. In a place that gets 280 inches of precipitation a year (rain, sleet, or snow, but generally all three at once), these things are a fact of life.

But I didn't know these things that first morning. What I did know was that it was getting light and that it was time to wander out to the beach and find out, officially, whether hawks were foolish enough to migrate in slush.

Ted Swem, a research biologist for BIRS (pronounced "beers"), snored gently in the next Polarguard bag over. The bag was in a puddle. We were doing a hawk migration study funded jointly by the U.S. Fish and Wildlife Service and the Bureau of Land Management. Little is known about hawk migration in Alaska; in fact, almost nothing. Ted Swem and Bob Dittrick had studied topographic maps of the southeast coast of Alaska and noticed that at one point, some forty miles north of Yakutat, the Malispina Glacier edges down to the Gulf of Alaska. Assuming that birds of prey are not tickled at the prospect of crossing a Rhode Island-sized chunk of sterile ice, it looked like a natural migratory bottleneck—a trap between water and ice—providing, of course, that birds of prey even *followed* the Alaska coast.

Like I said, there are a lot of unknowns.

So Bob and Ted floated a proposal. The idea was intriguing, the price was right, and bingo, the project was on. And if Dittrick hadn't gotten bogged down developing nature centers for the state of Alaska, which forced a reluctant call for immigrant labor from New Jersey, you wouldn't be reading about it in these pages.

"I think I'll go see what time hawks get up around here," I said for openers.

The snoring stopped.

"All right," Ted said agreeably.

"How'd you sleep?" I inquired, stalling for time.

There was a long pause. "All right. It was sorta cold, though."

"Yeah, it was cold," I agreed. "But not real cold," I added, bravely.

"No, not real cold," Ted agreed, just as bravely.

There followed a lengthy silence. So much for openers.

"Well, I guess I'll get up," I said again. Ted agreed that this was a good idea. And since there was no one to contradict him, I got up.

We had flown into Yakutat on 18 April aboard an Air Alaska 727, which is a lot like other jets but smaller. For three uneventful but expensive days we had idled in the lounge of the Glacier Bear Motel waiting to see which would come first, clear skies or exhausted funds. That was four days ago. On 20 April, our bush pilot gave us the go-ahead. After a forty-minute flight around snow squalls and over a dark and unfriendly Gulf of Yakutat, in a plane held together with duct tape and blind faith, we touched down on Sitkagi Beach. That was yesterday.

At the door to the tent, I reached back and extracted a pocket-sized waterproof notebook, a Remington riot gun loaded with slugs, and my Griz-Kit. A Griz-Kit is a sort of backcountry comfort blanket. Its working parts consist of a plastic traveler's soap container, three M-80 firecrackers, a Bic lighter, and a cigar. If charged by griz: (1) open soap box, (2) light cigar, (3) ignite M–80 by holding fuse to cigar and inhaling deeply, and (4) throw lit M–80 at irate grizzly.

Ted assured me that it works—providing, of course, you have at your disposal the time it takes to complete steps one through four. If your fingers are stiff with cold (which they always are) and the wind keeps blowing out your lighter (which it always does), then the process might take a little longer.

Hence, the Remington riot gun.

Now, griz is a pretty even-tempered critter, but there were several things working against a friendly encounter at Sitkagi. First, it was spring, and a grizzly fresh out of hibernation is on the cranky side. Second, he is apt to be hungry and that makes him crankier. Third, if "he" is a she, she might have cubs, and that makes her protective and a little on edge. Fourth, coastal fishermen think it is loads of fun to throw lead at bears on the beach at outrageous distances (like three to four hundred yards). Coastal bears, especially those that are carrying samples of that lead under their hides, don't think this is particularly funny; a few might even bear a grudge. And, finally, about seventy yards from where we were watching hawks on Sitkagi Beach there was a nice, ripe, sea lion carcass—*exactly* the kind of tide-me-by that griz is looking for when he is fresh out of a five-month fast.

And he might not be keen on sharing it.

So, at the door I reached into my right pant's pocket and removed my wallet containing all the essentials fit for survival in Twentieth Century America—credit cards, driver's license, currency—and replaced it with something tailored to survival needs at Sitkagi: my Griz-Kit.

There was fresh ice on the feeder stream that lay between the sleeping camp and the cooking camp, and there would be every morning of our stay. The cooking camp was as we had left it the night before; equipment lashed to the trunks in case we had misjudged the intensity of the tides, food stashed in buckets up in trees in case *Ursus* felt porcine.

I broke through the sharp wall of spruce onto open beach. There was no transition. One instant I was in deep woods; the next, on open beach. Looking east and west until my sight grew thin in needle spray and ice rain, I surveyed Sitkagi. Before me were fifty yards of coarse volcanic sand and, beyond, a dark churning turbulence called the Gulf of Alaska. In the surf, seemingly immune from all harm, were scores of Mew Gulls snatching bits of kelp torn loose from their sea beds by the violence of the waves.

The night tide had erased all trace of our arrival: wheel marks, footpads, the drag marks from heavy equipment. Sitkagi looked like the world on the sixth day, before the Creator opted to gamble on one last addition.

I stepped from the trees, scattered fifteen or twenty Bald Eagles (the starlings of Sitkagi) from the defunct sea lion, and headed for the shelter (*sic*) of the overhanging hemlock that was to be our watch point. I didn't expect to see any hawks. *Not even a Gyrfalcon*, I reasoned, *would fly in a slush storm.* But migration in coastal Alaska doesn't wait for good weather. If it did, birds probably wouldn't breed until August. Hundreds of Canada, White-fronted, and Snow Geese were on the move.

141

Occasionally, pushed by a blistering tailwind, small flocks of Trumpeter and Tundra Swans took form in the swirling gray backdrop and sped down the beach.

In my two weeks at Sitkagi, a spring migration unfolded, a full spring compressed into thirteen days. Time is of the essence in Alaska, where summer days are long but the season short. During the first part of the project, waterfowl were the migratory mainstays—this is like March in Cape May. But by the third of May, it was bull-market shorebirds: Western Sandpipers, turnstone, Dunlin, Black-bellied Plover all going by at a rate of two hundred per minute—this is like May at home. And there were large, gangly flocks of Sandhill Cranes, three hundred at a clip, four thousand a day, their calls sounding like a thousand ungreased wooden hinges—but we don't have Sandhills at Cape May.

And we don't have weather like they brew in the Aleutians and throw at Sitkagi—at least not that you would go out in. But we do have hawks at Cape May, and in this regard, for the first hour that I spent at Sitkagi Beach in the sleet, Cape May had it all over Sitkagi. A whistle from Ted, shrill enough to be heard over the surf and sleet and the chatter of teeth, was like a reprieve from the gallows.

Over the steaming (but fast cooling) mug of coffee, Ted looked mildly out of sorts—which is the most severe display of ill-humor that Ted allows himself.

"Seen any migratory raptorial-type birds?" he inquired.

"Nope. Lots of waterfowl, though," I said, trying to sound cheerful.

Ted seemed to ponder this a while. Something was eating him.

"The stove is throwing a tantrum," he allowed, finally, unable to carry the burden by himself any longer, trusting that I could take it. "It sort of throws a flame twenty feet in the air and then simmers down to a wimpy little thing that wouldn't warm donkey dung.

"And it is burning an *incredible* lot of fuel," he added as an afterthought.

This was the worst of all possible bad news. In the field,

things come right down to elementals. Happiness is being warm and dry and well fed. By the nature of our situation, pleasure generators numbers one and two were out of reach. But the thought of cold rations to boot was ill fortune beyond all bearing.

It was at this bleak moment that I pulled back my head to drain the mug and there, thirty feet over Ted's wet watch cap, was:

1 NH, AHYF, head. W, Par. B, #2—or as roughly translated: one Northern Harrier, after-hatching-year female, heading West, parallel to beach at moderate height.

There was no time for witty remarks. Elemental situations give rise to elemental expressions of feeling.

"Look. Look. Over your head. Behind you. Look. Harrier! Look, harrier!"

Ted spun around like a phalarope on amphetamines and chanted—"Alll Riiight. Alll Right! Northern-God-DAMN-*Circus cyaenus* HARRIER! ALLL RIGHT!"

And so now we had concrete evidence that both Bob and Ted had guessed right. Maybe hawks *did* migrate along Sitkagi Beach, in the sleet, when they should be sitting; heading west, when all reason says that they should be going north.

And they *had* guessed right, raptor folks that they are. Hawks really do migrate at Sitkagi. Certainly the migration there can't compare, volume for volume, with the Cape May flight, or even with a Sandy Hook flight. But for drama and quality, Sitkagi's hawk flight is a cut above the pack.

First, we had to develop a whole new sense for relative abundance. The common raptor migrant at Sitkagi is the harrier. The Sharp-shinned Hawk, migratory mainstay on the Atlantic Coast, is a poor second. Second, though flights are highly weather-related (just as they are at other hawk watch sites) everything seems to work in reverse. At Sitkagi, if there is nasty, rotten weather, there are hawks. Ted and I got used to the idea of the "pre-squall flight," the "post-squall flight," and even the "mid-squall flight." If, on the other hand, there is a nice bright sunny day, there are no hawks. Under these conditions, raptors leave the beach and catch thermals inland.

Rough-legged Hawk

Of course, what this meant was that observations were most important when the weather was severely inclement. And inclement weather on the Alaskan coast is about the rudest thing imaginable.

Our working understanding of the mechanics of the Sitkagi flight was not instantaneous. It wasn't like sauntering up to the North Lookout of Hawk Mountain and having the sages hand you a game plan whose basic elements were understood back when hawk watching was conducted over the barrels of twelve-gauge doubles. No, we earned the twelve hundred—odd birds we saw during our thirteen days at Sitkagi. And more important, we learned.

In the evenings, we'd bring our folding lawn chairs out onto the beach (our one concession to creature comfort) and watch evening-soft skies for late harriers or early Short-eared Owls.

Maybe Ted would dig out his pipe and smoke a celebratory bowl, maybe we'd talk over the day's flight, or maybe we'd simply watch as tall shadows reached for the water's edge.

And I recall thinking, on my last evening at Sitkagi, that this is how it was once at Hawk Mountain, at Cape May, at Raccoon Ridge, and at those other famous and established hawk watch sites. That Ted and I now shared a bond of kinship with those grand masters—the Brouns, the Saunders, and the Edwards of this world, who pioneered these mighty migratory junctions. These men whose names are legends.

And I learned something, I think, about legends at Sitkagi.

When I walked down to the water's edge with dishes that needed washing, I carried this new-found understanding with me and I turned it over in my mind the way a sea otter might tease the secrets from a brightly colored stone. And that's when I picked up the skipper, couched in comfort and kinship with those other stones that rolled in the surf at Sitkagi. And it was smooth and round and it felt good, like a thought complete. And I held it for a long time in long debate before putting it in my pocket.

In the morning I took the Griz-Kit out of my pocket and traded it for a three-fold wallet. But the skipper came with me to Cape May. So it could sit on my desk, for a time. So I could look at it as I wrote this story.

And now, the story is over and I can finish my task because I intend to take that stone and put it back in my pocket. I will walk down to Cape May Point. It is slack tide. The bay is windless and glassy. I have been waiting for such a day since my return.

I am going to wander down to the water's edge and with all the borrowed skill that memory can muster, I am going to hold my stone, pointer finger to thumb, and start it back on its way to Sitkagi.

Macadam Encounter

I picked up a hitchhiker one March; it's a habit of mine. Altruism wasn't the motive. An unholy backlog of riding debts incurred during a wanderlust youth weigh heavy on me. Guilt is a peerless motivator, and the fact that there were but five more miles of driveable roadway left (before I hit water) salved me with the assurance that if the fellow was a zealot from some nut-fringe religious sect or someone going through life with only one oar in the water, at least I wouldn't have to humor him for long.

Some hitchhikers, neophytes by and large, feel that a ride must be paid for in conversation. Others, veterans, feel comfortable dispensing with the song and dance if silence suits their host.

This fellow fell into the former category. In answer to one of the stock questions governing such meetings ("Where ya from?"), I received an enthusiastic tale that might be titled: "The Life and Times of a Wahoo West Virginny Boy Come to the Bright Lights."

This macadam encounter would concern us a great deal less than it already does were it not for something my companion said. Taking advantage of a rare break in the spilling of events, I asked him whether he ever missed his home state. He replied, "Oh, it's boring as hell down here in the winter and working at the fish docks is a drag. But, man, oh man, who could ever leave Wildwood in the summer?"

I thought it expedient not to answer.

His words stayed with me because they brought to mind the grand diversity of our species. You see, nothing short of persuasion at gunpoint could get me *into* Wildwood in the summer. Summer to me is the lingering gold of long evenings, legions of shorebirds weaving a pattern of hesitation between flight and alight and then disappearing into a veiled horizon. Summer to my friend was penny arcades, video games, bright lights, and bourbon laughter. That's not my ken, and splitting the two of us into separate species on the basis of habitat selection seemed a weak justification—not that it hasn't been done. Like starlings and coyotes, our species seems capable of acclimating to a variety of haunts.

Yesterday I sat with clipboard and binoculars at South Cape May and watched the hard-pressed remnants of a once thriving

Piping Plover

Least Tern colony. Sandwiched between a mosaic of beach towels, their backs up against the dunes, the birds were making a stand.

I watched the males' display, the airborne courtship, the pair-bonding ritual and mused at the parallels in our own species—display on the beach, courtship in the bar, on the dance floor, and so forth. The difference? Only in terms of success. Our species increases; the terns do not.

And I could not help but feel a sense of sadness for the birds, outplayed by a more aggressive species, my species. But science offers solace, and I am reminded that species have succeeded other species on this planet ever since we ran out of easy niches to fill. Dying, after all, is just as *natural* as living—merely different. And so is extinction!

As different as night and day.

As different as bright lights and bourbon laughter, and legions of shorebirds disappearing into a veiled horizon.

Thoughts While Waiting for an Ice Falcon

The wind turned dirty and easterly sometime during the night. The temperature has been falling all morning.

Driven mist hurdles the top of the hawk watch platform, tatters into ghost banners through the railing, and passes on. Sometimes it thins enough to reveal dark forms and the soft glow of lights that are the town of Cape May. They aren't necessary. I know where the town lies just as well as I know where my hand must fall to find the binoculars suspended from my neck. These things are etched in memory. Five years at Cape May Point have seen to that.

"So, how many hours have we spent watching hawks from this spot?"

"I don't know. Three thousand, maybe four."

"And how many do you suppose we've seen?"

"Three hundred thousand or so, maybe more—check the records if you're so curious. And what makes *you* so talkative today? Have I been bad or are you just bored from lack of work?"

"Sorry, old pal," my inner voice purred, *"record-keeping is your job. Why should I work your side of the Id? But now that you are paying me half a mind (so to speak), just what are we doing out here anyway? There hasn't been a hawk flight worthy of the name since the last week in November. Nothing is going to move in this arctic gruel; you couldn't see it if it did. What's more, it is cold enough to freeze an eider. . . ."*

There was a short, uneasy pause catered to let these several considerations weaken the support struts of my resolve; it was

149

followed by the haymaker of undermining alternatives: *"Be-sides, there is work to do back at the office."*

"I'm using up vacation time, remember?" I challenged, stung.

"You have work to do," my inner voice repeated, pressing its advantage.

"It'll get done," I said, rallying. "I'll work tonight."

And again, *"You have work to do."*

"Let's wait a bit. We'll go after a bit."

The town of Cape May

"And just what are we waiting for?"
"I don't know," I said, evasively. "Nothing probably," I lied.
"Just waiting."

The bird will come down the beach because that is the nature of its kind—*because that is how I want to see it.* It will be
a day like this one, unremittingly cold, gray without hope, like
the world that lies on the far side of despair.
It will have spent the night on Long Island Sound (having fed

heavily on a Black Duck that had judged legal hunting time to have ended and foolishly lifted off the marsh unmindful of more skilled and ancient enemies). Sunset will catch it still on the tidal flats and it will have roosted locally, maybe on the skeletal remains of some bayman's skiff, long grounded and forgotten even by the man who built it. At first light, it will lift off and head due south over open water, into rain that changes to sleet, then to snow, and back to rain as the miles stretch behind it.

The weather will trouble it little, likewise the quartering winds that carry it landward. Though this bird is a machine tuned to a perfection of flight beyond our comprehension, even the finest of machines must be fueled. It will grow hungry again, make landfall near Atlantic City, perhaps, and although the flock of Brant that lift off in panic before it can claim lineage to ancestors as adept at surviving as the Ice Falcon can at killing, one young bird with a wing recently damaged by shot cannot make the cut. While the falcon feeds, the surviving Brant will do likewise, the encounter mutually forgotten by both parties.

In the distance, cars move along a raised dike, stop occasionally to disgorge passengers who seem to search for something, and then move on. In the poor light, the Ice Falcon looks like just another piece of weathered wood. It goes unseen.

The hawk watch platform glistens with the newness of fresh-cut pine varnished with a coat of mist. Last October, eager faces lined the rail, but the platform is empty now.

Because of the weather.

Because of the season.

Empty.

It's cold.

The wind is rising. The foxtail shiver but the water droplets refuse to be shaken loose. Frozen.

Visibility has improved, though. Cape May stands stark and mute across the marsh and the jagged gulf where the village of South Cape May stood thirty years ago. In town, there is gaiety and laughter despite the weather. The shopper's mall is bustling with last-minute gift buying. The Ugly Mug is glowing with warmth and good cheer only traceable in part to the contents of the cups. But none of this is visible from the hawk watch platform.

I'm cold.

After resting and preening, the Ice Falcon will lift off and fly low and direct across the marsh, a broad avenue of familiarity, comfortably open, bordered by tangled woods on the west and unbroken development to the east. The bird will climb leisurely, level off at two hundred feet, just below the ceiling, and eat up miles with steady wing beats.

Behind Wildwood, there will be a waterfowler I know. He hunts in these conditions. He will have just limited out and will be leaning over the side of his cedar sneak box and hooking anchor lines on the dekes with an outstreched oar. The Ice Falcon passing overhead will go unnoticed except by the dark-eyed German Shorthair in the bow, who will observe its passage with quiet interest.

The mist has become a fine driving rain that seeps through my parka and its space-age fabric with ease. My wool watch cap must have reached its saturation threshold, too. A cold trickle of water glances behind an ear, threads down the nape of my neck, warms gradually, and loses itself in wet anonymity to several layers of wool sweater.

"Yeah, I'll say the parka is waterproof. Rain goes right through the fabric, soaks you to the marrow, and it remains as dry as the day it came off the assembly line. Now, that's what I call technology!

"I don't suppose you kept the warranty card, did you?"

"No."

"I thought not. You didn't, perhaps, just read it, did you?"

I take a scan along the tree line, over the marsh, to the dunes, the town beyond, and the open bay beyond that; silence serves for an answer. I don't get off that easy—but after a lifetime's association, I really didn't expect to.

"You know," my inner voice persisted, *"it's not like we have to be here. The hawk watch officially ended four weeks ago."*

"I know. I signed the contract, remember?"

"Oh, sure, but did you read it?"

(I'm forced to smile.) "I read it."

"No kidding?"

"Yeah, no kidding."

There was a short, suspicious pause.

"Say, how about dropping into the park office and begging a cup of coffee? You know—to warm up a bit."

Bribery!

"You can still keep an eye out of the window if you want."

A well-thought-out bribe, too. I'm tempted, sorely, but not persuaded.

"But I can't use binoculars through the windows, too much distortion. Let's give it another minute or so."

The Ice Falcon will probably be quite close before I see it, naked-eye close. But I will pick it up with my glasses first. Not because of the weather or the many, many gulls that draw and dull your attention during December at Cape May Point, but because year by year I rely more and more upon binoculars to locate birds—compensation for eyes that just don't seem able to pick up birds as quickly as they used to. Six years of searching harsh morning suns have taken their toll.

The foxtail bow lower, burdened by ice. A Yellow-rumped Warbler lands on the platform, hops along the rail. It is wet, no doubt hungry. Only hunger could have forced it out of the protecting bayberry on a day like this.

A sharp gust makes it lean forward with half-closed eyes. There is no footing for small feet. It slides backward, loses the rail, chirps once, and spins crazily into the bayberry.

Something wet and heavy touches my face. Large flakes are mixing with the rain, melting where they touch the ground but clinging and building on the foxtail. The driving will be treacherous tonight.

I have never seen an Ice Falcon, though I might have, several times, if I had wanted to "chase" a sighting.

Somebody else's sighting.

They are regular enough in New England, just eight hours away, and they occur closer than that on occasions. No, I want to see this bird here and I want to find it myself. It will mean more that way and I don't want to cheat it. Though I have been tempted many times, though I will compromise other things, I don't want to cheat this sighting, not this one.

I hope it is a gray bird, a female. Most people, I guess, would hope for a white bird, but the odds are against it. I will be happy enough with a gray bird. But it will probably be a young bird, a dark one—coffee-colored.

"Ahem, about that coffee?"

"In a minute."

"Well, what do you say to a fast run up the beach in the meantime—to keep our fuel lines from icing up?"

"In a minute. A couple of more scans, first."

I don't think I will have any trouble recognizing the bird when I see it. There are only two birds that it might be confused with: a Peregrine and, under the right circumstances, a Goshawk. I have seen many of these.

No, identification won't be the problem.

It will come down the beach and it will be quite close before I see it. A large dark falcon, the color of woodsmoke. The tail will be wider than the lesser falcon's, the body will be heavy and the wings broader, more rounded than a Peregrine's. The flight will be direct and fast; the wing beats fast and shallow—almost as if all motion were confined to the wing-tips alone. The face will be dark.

I'd like very much for the bird to perch briefly so I can study it, or at least to circle once or twice. But that is asking much of an Ice Falcon, too much. Twelve miles of open water won't pose any deterrent. When the beach begins to curl west, rounding the Point, the bird will lose patience and strike off across Delaware Bay low and fast, a gray shadow swallowed swiftly by

155

water and sky. A minute will be all that I'll have, if I'm lucky.

I don't know how the world will change after I see it. Probably nothing will change. There will always be another bird to find, another ideal to replace this one, just a little farther out of reach. I'll worry about it after I see it. If I see it.

If I'm very, very lucky.

"Listen, just for the novelty of it, let's try self-immolation next time. It's quicker."

"No, there aren't any fires allowed in the park—and besides, we're too wet to burn."

The attempt at humor is not well received.

"JEEZUS CHRIST ON A BOBSLED, MAN, LET'S PACK IT IN. WE . . . ARE . . . FREEZING. AND, WE ARE GOING TO DIE HERE!"

I sigh, glance quickly at my watch. It reads 3:25.

"All right, just five more minutes. We'll leave in five minutes. Just lay off for a bit, now; I want to do a scan."

I slip the rain guard off and bring the very worn, very familiar binoculars quickly to my eyes. My hand, closing gently around the lenses, form a cup to protect them. The world swirls dark and gray.

A large, gray-backed bird, cloaked in snow, passes quickly through the field and disappears behind the dunes. I move the glasses ahead to a break where the bird must pass into the open—but find both lenses hopelessly fogged. The bird clears the opening low and fast, riding the updraft on swept-back wings. I can get nothing on it before it passes out of sight again.

I sprint, stiff-legged because of the ice, the length of the platform (trusting the rail to stop me). I lick both objective lenses to clear them of snow and bring them up to the point where the bird should emerge. Split seconds hang in suspension. *It's been too long,* I think. *The bird should have been out in the open by now. It must have altered course. Maybe it's down on the deck too low to see. I'm going to miss it!*

Then it's out; blurred but identifiable.

Adult Herring Gull.

I glance at my watch but have trouble reading it. My hands are shaking. No doubt, from the cold. It's 3:30.

"OK. That's it. Let's go. Bit of excitement there at the end. Had you guessing there for a minute, eh? What'd ya think it was?"

I glance down at the watch again, up the beach, to the sky, and back to the watch.

"OK—we'll call it a day. Just one more scan or so."

"No way! You said '3:30.' You promised 3:30. No way."

"Sure, sure," I sooth, "take it easy, just one last scan, that's all. It's a tradition at hawk watches. You know that. The one final scan. . . ."

Five seconds pass . . . ten . . . (I think he's biting) . . .

"One last scan?"

"That's all," I say in a fashion that would put even the most doubtful mind at ease.

. . . fifteen . . . twenty . . .

"No lie?"

(He's biting. Twenty-nine years of keeping me straight and he's still biting.)

"God's honest truth."

"All right. But that's it! One last scan. Promise?"

"Promise," I say half aloud.

The lights glow brighter in town but the distance robs them of warmth. There is no sound except for the hiss of snow on the water and rush of waves breaking on the beach. The world swirls in soft confusion; the waves sound as if they are breaking all around. It's snowing harder now.